Chesapeake Ferries

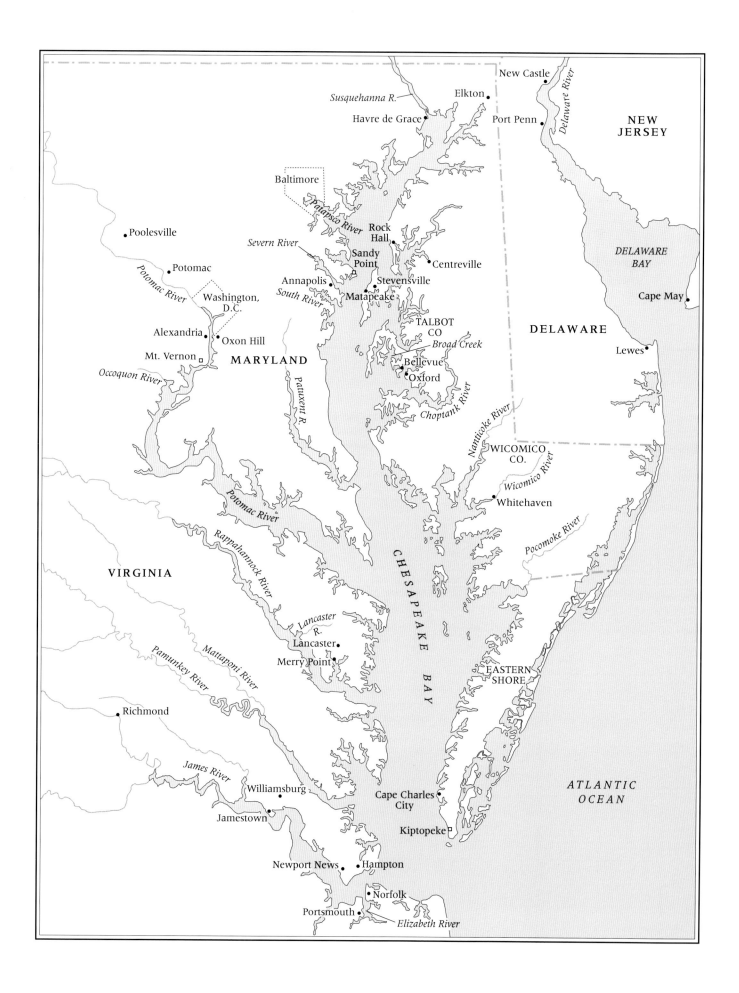

Chesapeake Ferries

A Waterborne Tradition, 1636–2000

CLARA ANN SIMMONS

MARYLAND HISTORICAL SOCIETY

BALTIMORE, MARYLAND • 2009

Maryland Historical Society
201 W. Monument Street
Baltimore, Maryland 21201

Publication of this work was made possible by the generous support
of the Friends of the Press of the Maryland Historical Society.

ISBN 0-938420-78-x

Manufactured in the United States of America.
The paper used in this book meets the minimum requirements of the
American National Standard for Information Sciences Permanence of Paper
For Printed Library Materials, ANSI Z39.48-1984.

This book is printed on acid-free paper.

Library of Congress Cataloging-in-Publication Data

Simmons, Clara Ann, 1923–2008
    Chesapeake ferries : a waterborne tradition, 1636–2000 / Clara Ann Simmons.
        p.   cm.
    Includes bibliographical references and index.
    ISBN 0-938420-78-X (alk. paper)
    1. Ferries—Virginia. 2. Ferries—Maryland. I. Title.
    HE5783.V8S56 2009
    386'.60916347—dc22
                                              2008052738

Contents

Preface

Shortly after I moved to the Eastern Shore of Maryland, almost fifty years ago, a new-found friend introduced me to the Oxford-Bellevue Ferry in Talbot County, and I was hooked. Not necessarily on ferries, but coming from the mountains I marveled at this land of rivers and creeks and bays, and knew this was where I wanted to stay.

As time went on, I began to write articles on the maritime way of life of the early settlers who went everywhere by water. I was fascinated by the aplomb with which young men went to sea at an early age, and by the matter-of-fact use of ships and boats by people of all ages. Eventually this led to trips to extant ferries and interest in extinct ones. What follows is an informal history, from 1636 to 2000, of tidewater Chesapeake Bay ferries, although a few well-known non-tidal ones are listed or described. By ferries, I mean boats that set the traveler on his way so that he might continue his journey. The exceptions are the cross-harbor ferries of Norfolk and Baltimore, that served commuters. I have not included steam ferries that ran one-day excursions to amusement parks and beaches. Steam ferries which connected with a railroad that went to a beach are included; they were used by day trippers in the summertime, but provided transportation for many people the year around.

During the age of sail, ferries proliferated, often being just a few miles apart. They usually went from one plantation wharf to another, frequently changed hands so that different names would apply to the same crossing and in some cases only existed for a few years. Some of them, for which we have information, became major crossing points for colonial travel. For others, such as the small steam ferries that plied the creeks and rivers, there remains but a tantalizing hint. If their owners kept records, very few have survived.

Writing a history requires the help of many people. I am especially indebted to the courteous, knowledgeable, mostly volunteer staffs of county historical societies. They quickly responded and often provided additional pertinent information.

Especially helpful to me were Mabel E. Andrews of the Historical Society of Harford County, Bel Air, Maryland; Michael L. Dixon of the Historical Society of Cecil County, Elkton, Maryland; Robert G. Miller of the Columbia Historic Preservation Society, Columbia, Pennsylvania; John W. Royal of the Woodland Ferry Association, Woodland, Delaware; George K. Combs, Lloyd House, Alexandria, Virginia; and Darlene Tallent of the Westmoreland County Museum and Library, Montross, Virginia. I have been aided by the staffs of the Mariners' Museum, Newport News, Virginia; the Chesapeake Bay Maritime Museum, St. Michaels, Maryland; the Eastern Shore Public Library, Accomac, Virginia; the Queen Anne's County Free Library, Centreville, Maryland; Clifton M. Miller Library, Washington College, Chestertown, Maryland; the Maryland State Archives, Annapolis, Maryland; the Maryland Historical Society, Baltimore, Maryland; the Norfolk Historical Society, Norfolk, Virginia; researcher Virginia Philips; and Darcey Schoeninger, Queen Anne's County Arts Council, Centreville, Maryland.

I give a nod of thanks to the diarists down through the centuries who described their times, often more abbreviated than one would wish, that add that personal touch to history. I hope their genre continues in this age of instant communication.

I thank my family, Elisabeth, Ellen, and Kenneth for their support, humorous and serious, but always steadfast.

Clara Ann Simmons passed away before her book went to press. Chesapeake Ferries *is being published in her memory by Elisabeth M. Simmons and Ellen C. Simmons as a tribute to their mother, her research, and her work.*

The editors wish to thank Dr. Pete Lesher, curator of collections at the Chesapeake Bay Maritime Museum, for his updates and thoughtful suggestions.

PREFACE

Chesapeake Ferries

CHAPTER 1

Settlement and Growth in the Virginia Tidewater

"A verie goodly Bay"

The Chesapeake Bay is an estuary unique in the world's geology. Formed from the bed of an ancient river, it has forty-eight principal tributaries.[1] The names of many, derivatives of Native American names, roll off the tongue—Susquehanna, Rappahannock, Potomac, Patapsco, Patuxent, Wicomico, Occoquan. Others reflect the area's English heritage: Lynnhaven, James, York, Elizabeth. Estuaries meet the rivers, such as the St. Mary's, Wicomico, Port Tobacco, Nanjemoy, Mattawoman, and Piscataway that run into the Potomac on its Maryland, or western, side. Breton and St. Clement's Bays empty there also, eons-old evidence that the tidewater area is crisscrossed with hundreds of creeks, inlets, and small bays. To get from one neck of land to another one must cross a body of water, large or small. One must cross harbors in order to travel through some cities in the Virginia and Maryland tidewater, and the Chesapeake Bay itself divides parts of both states. It is no wonder that in 1621, fourteen years after the founding of Jamestown, Governor Sir Francis Wyatt and the Council of Virginia requested their sponsor, the London Company, to send shipbuilders, for without "Shipps, Pynnaces, and small vessels" they could not explore new land, seek trade with their neighbors, or "Transporte eyther ourselves, or our Goodes from one Place to

Smith's Map of Virginia, 1608.

another."[2] Water was the settlers' highway. Riding along it and ferrying across it they developed a system of travel that reached its sailing zenith in the eighteenth century and continued via steam in the nineteenth. Water travel continues today via a few scattered, nostalgic, motorized relics.

Early explorers of the New World seem to have been unaware of the Chesapeake Bay. Several skirted the bay; and some entered the bay and got as far as the Potomac River, but they did not mention the vast expanse of water. In 1570 a group of Spanish Jesuits sailed up the James River in search of a site for a mission. Fifteen years later, John White's 1585 map showing the bay and four rivers on its western side was published in England. John White traveled as the artist on the expedition led by Sir Walter Raleigh, and his map must have caused excitement when it first appeared. Captain John Smith was the first European known to navigate the entire length of the Chesapeake Bay and map his findings. Smith probably knew of White's map before he sailed with the London Company in 1607 to settle this new land.

The London Company had received its charter from King James I in April 1606 and therefore had license to begin settlements in the area between 34° and 41° north latitude. The company hoped that precious metals such as gold and copper would be discovered and, above all, that new-found waterways would lead to a passage to India and the riches therein. Members of the company, eager for a return on their investment, sailed in less than a year, on December 19, 1606. The hundred-ton *Susan Constant*, the forty-ton *Godspeed*, and the twenty-ton *Discovery* set sail under the leadership of Captain Christopher Newport, who chose the southern route to take advantage of the north equatorial current that flowed to the West Indies. From there the small flotilla took advantage of the Gulf Stream and sailed north to find a safe anchorage. On April 26, 1607, the ships rounded the entrance to a wondrous, broad bay and went ashore on the western cape to give thanks for their safe deliverance after more than four months of tedious travel. They named the spot Cape Henry in honor of King James I's eldest son. They named the opposite shore Cape Charles in honor of his second son. In his history of North American exploration and settlement, published in 1624, John Smith wrote, "There is but one entrance by Sea into this country and that is at the mouth of a verie goodly Bay, the widenesse whereof is neere eighteene or twenty miles."[3]

On May 13, after having explored the area from their anchorage on Cape Henry, the three small ships sailed up the newly named James River. On a peninsula surrounded by water deep enough to enable them to moor their boats to the trees, and which promised protection from marauding natives, they established their colony. The company appointed a council of thirteen to govern, one of whom was twenty-seven-year-old Captain John Smith. Since the age of fifteen, Smith had spent his life as a sailor, soldier, and adventurer. During that first summer at Jamestown, Smith set out to explore a nearby river, the Chickahominy. He was captured by an Indian hunting party, paraded from Indian settlement to Indian settlement, and finally taken to the great chief Powhatan, who saved his life. Smith wrote much later of the chief's daughter, Pocahontas.

The first winter was grueling, and no doubt Smith thought of the "goodly bay" that promised a roadway to riches. The little colony had suffered famine, fire, severe cold, and attacks by the natives. Only about sixty of the original 105 settlers lived to welcome the spring of 1608.[4]

In June of 1608 Smith set out from Jamestown with fourteen men in an open barge to explore and chart all of the waters he could. The party consisted of six gentlemen, four soldiers, one doctor, a blacksmith, a fishmonger, and a fisherman. Smith and his party left seemingly unprepared for the humid heat and hot July sun, and traveled in an open boat that offered no protection. They also suffered the sudden gusts and squalls (the bane of many a future ferryman) that suddenly blew up on the rivers and bay, yet seemed surprised when they first encountered a quick storm. They first sailed to the Eastern Shore, where they lost their mast during a sudden rainstorm, and Smith wrote that they were lucky to have escaped the "unmerciful raging of that ocean-like water."[5]

During their first exploratory voyage of the bay, a seven-week trip, the group encountered hostile natives and suffered illness. They lacked fresh water, and ate water-logged, spoiled bread. With no means to live off the land, they once tried to catch fish with a frying pan, although one wonders if Richard Keale, the fishmonger, and Jonas Profit, the fisherman, embarked without hook, line, and sinker to provide food for the foray. Smith's history, published many years after his adventures, is embellished with fanciful and heroic tales.

Despite their difficulties, Smith sailed the barge as far north as the Patapsco River, a waterway he named the Bolus because of the red clay found on its banks. On their return trip they entered the Potomac and ascended it as far as "we could with the bote," e.g., to the fall line where the coastal plain meets the Piedmont Plateau and the water drops to sea level. They took yet another detour on the way home and explored the Rappahannock River for a distance of more than one hundred miles. This river so teemed with fish that when the ship became grounded because of an ebb tide, the crew speared them with swords. In just thirty short years after this exploratory trip, ferries began to cross the long Potomac, and between 1638 and 1815 over one hundred sail- or hand-operated craft plied the river daily.

Smith and his crew returned to Jamestown on July 21, 1608, and three days later he set out again, this time with thirteen men, seven of them veterans of the first adventure, to explore the "Bay of Chisiapiake" as far north as possible. When they arrived at the head of the bay they met the mighty Susquehannock Indians and the equally powerful river bearing their name, Susquehanna. Smith found that rocks and low water stopped his shallop and he could not sail far up the river, but the Indian "cannows" could go farther.

The Indians used bark and dugout canoes and taught the explorers how to make the latter by burning out more than half of the top section of a log. These canoes proved invaluable for early travel and much later would be made any desired size by joining and caulking two or more hollowed logs. Settlers in these early days often used canoes as ferryboats and rowed or poled passengers across an estuary while their horses swam alongside.

Smith explored some of the major rivers of the eastern side of the bay and returned to Jamestown on September 7, 1608. The riches he had found consisted of endless waterways, lands of fertile soil, and abundant timber, game, and fish. He also found hostile Indians, but those on the Eastern Shore, then called the Kingdom of Accomack, were friendly. His reports led other explorers to navigate the Chesapeake, and slowly colonization of the area began. In the spring of 1634, Leonard Calvert, in command of the *Ark* and the *Dove*, sailed between Capes Henry and Charles into Chesapeake Bay and up the Potomac River to an island on the eastern side of the river that he named St. Clement's. Calvert had come to settle the proprietary colony that King Charles I had granted to his brother Cecilius Calvert, Lord Baltimore, in April 1632. After a scouting trip, Leonard Calvert moved his colonists down the Potomac to a branch he named the St. Mary's River and there, at the site of an abandoned Indian village, they built St. Mary's

The first landing of Leonard Calvert, as imagined by David Acheson Woodward, ca. 1865–1870.

City, capital of the new province, Maryland. Colonization along the rivers, creeks, and bay continued and remained the norm for many years. The settlers needed easy access to travel. There were, of course, grants of thousands of acres and large plantations developed, but most settlers bought or rented farms of approximately one hundred acres. Settlement density along the water is seen in a 1641 survey of St. Clement's Hundred on the Wicomico River on Maryland's Western Shore. Seven years after settling the Maryland colony, 90 percent of the households stood along the water.[6]

John Smith's report, bereft of instant riches, prompted the London Company to search for export items other than the clapboards, tobacco, and tar the Virginians had been sending to England. In an effort to capitalize on natural resources, Captain Samuel Argyll of Jamestown sailed Governor Sir Thomas Dale across the bay to the tip of the Eastern Shore in 1612. They knew the land on the ocean side was full of islands with good meadows and they hoped they could make salt in shallow ponds. The area abounded in shellfish and cod that could be salted for export. The Virginians established a small settlement on the peninsula to produce salt and catch fish. Never profitable, the London Company discontinued the venture in 1619.[7] Five years later, in 1624, the Court of King's Bench in England withdrew the charter of the financially troubled London Company.

First to arrive on the bay, and due to the demands of the salt meadow experiment, Virginians began ferrying to, and colonizing, the Eastern Shore by the early 1620s. They settled for the most part on three waterways, Old Plantation Creek, King's Creek, and Cherrystone Creek. By 1635 settlers claimed all of the land along the water from Cape Charles to Old Plantation Creek. The alternative to water travel— foot travel (walking a path to the head of a creek)—was a much too time-consuming and tiring way to get from one side of a waterway to the other. People started moving about by dugout, shallop, or scow depending on the water to be crossed and the length of the trip.[8]

Flat-bottomed scows proved best for crossing narrow, protected waters and in time a prototype developed. This boat drew little water, had upright sides two or three feet in height, and sloped upward at each end. These sloping ends could be used as a gangplank as the ferry came to shore, sandy or otherwise. In some instances, the sloping ends could be lowered to make an apron for crossing onto land. The boats could be thirty feet long by eight feet wide and carry three to six horses as well as passengers. Rowing and poling provided locomotion. Four ferrymen who poled their boats were sketched by architect and engineer Benjamin Henry Latrobe in one of his crossings of the Susquehanna River in Maryland. [9]

Susquehanna ferrymen, as depicted in a watercolor by Benjamin Henry Latrobe in 1808.

Settlers also used cable, or rope ferries. A cable strung on a fixed line from shore to shore passed through pulleys attached on the scow's side. Using a notched heaver hooked to the cable, the ferryman pulled the boat across. Sometimes boats were pulled by horses walking round and round a capstan to which the rope had been attached. Bell's Ferry

The Elizabeth River near Norfolk,
Virginia, as painted on March 21, 1796.

across the Susquehanna River ran in the last decade of the eighteenth century and used two boats tied together. One boat carried passengers and cargo and the other boat had a horse-powered paddlewheel and auxiliary sails. This method of a paddlewheel turned by horse power was prevalent until the use of steam power became widespread in the early nineteenth century. Boatmen used sloops and small schooners to cross the large expanses of water, the Chesapeake Bay, and the lower Potomac. These sailing ferries could accommodate a number of men, horses, and carriages, and some had decks and sleeping accommodations.

Public ferrying broadened the range of travel. Accomack County, Virginia, supported ferries at an early date and one of the earliest ferries in the public record was that of William Ward. In 1634, the year Calvert and the Maryland colonists landed at St. Clement's Island, the Accomack County Court appointed Ward to operate a ferry across King's Creek. The court also gave Ward the power to seize the property of anyone not paying their ferriage. Forty years later the long arm of the law on the Eastern Shore stepped in again in a peculiar case. The court ordered John Pope, accused of fornication with Olive Eaton, to build a ferryboat within a month's time. If he did not do so, he was to receive forty lashes and acknowledge his sin at church service.[10] One assumes he built the boat. Both of these examples underscore the importance of ferry travel.

Another early Virginia record cites a ferry established in 1636 in present-day Princess Anne County by one Adam Thoroughgood.[11] Thoroughgood had come to Virginia in 1621 and returned to England a few years later to find a wife. He successfully courted Sarah Offley, who came with a good dowry. They returned to Virginia in 1628 with 105 people whose passage Adam Thoroughgood had paid, no doubt using Sarah's money. According to a headright system passed in 1618, he received fifty acres for each person he imported. Thoroughgood settled on the western bank of the Lynnhaven River, became a successful tobacco planter, and participated in civic affairs. The ferry he established across the Elizabeth River prospered and he later operated one across the Lynnhaven. Ferries still operate on the Elizabeth River between Portsmouth and Norfolk.

By the time Adam Thoroughgood established his ferry service, Virginia's population had reached nearly five thousand. Rudimentary roads developed along the rivers and through forest clearings, comfortable homes overlooked the James and York Rivers, and appointed justices of the peace set fixed rates for ferries. In 1661 the general assembly legalized slavery and thereby provided labor for establishing a one-crop tobacco economy. By this time Virginia had a population of forty thousand, but the absence of industry precluded the need for towns. Although shiploads of colonists kept arriving at both Maryland and Virginia, neither colony could boast a town, save for Virginia's Jamestown.

King Charles II of England wanted towns established, and he directed Governor Sir William Berkeley to build a town like Jamestown on the York, the Rappahannock, the Potomac, and the Eastern Shore, and specified the buildings to be erected.[12] The assembly reluctantly passed "An Act for Building a Towne," precursor of similar acts passed in the ensuing years. Tappahannock (then known as Hobbs Hole) on the Rappahannock, grew from this legislation and served as the county seat. Onancock, on the Eastern Shore, settled in 1681 on the peninsula formed by the bay and the northern and southern branches of Onancock Creek, also gained designation as seat of Accomack County. Norfolk, situated at the southern tip of the bay where the eastern and southern branches of the Elizabeth River form a peninsula, became a port town under this act. In 1691 a new act calling for fifteen sites for cities resulted in Hampton and York. Also established was the strategically placed West Point, situated where the Pamunkey and Mattaponi

Rivers converge to form the York. A plat of the town drawn about 1781 shows Dadler's Ferry across the Mattaponi and Brick House Ferry across the Pamunkey.[13] When towns were established under these acts, the land was surveyed and a plat drawn. The 1691 survey for York specified that it be located "beginning at the lower side of Smyths Creek and so running downward by the river towards the ferry."[14] An eighteenth-century plat for Portsmouth, opposite Norfolk, clearly shows the area for the "Publik Ferry." Underneath this is written: "From the corner to low water mark." [15] Clusters of houses evolved around common ferries and often these sites became towns. The majority of towns listed in the various acts, however, never materialized. Cobham on the James River is but one example. Connected by ferry to the capital, Jamestown, it flourished for only a short time. Perhaps Virginia's most important town act was the one of 1699 that established Williamsburg as the capital. Jamestown had burned once again and the colony wanted the seat of government moved to a "healthy proper and commodious place."[16]

CHAPTER 2

Emergence of a Ferry System in Virginia

"Relaxation and frequent refreshing"

Owners of waterfront plantations had private docks from which they sallied forth to church, market, or friends' homes in brightly painted barges often manned by liveried servants. Those not fortunate enough to travel thus had to rely on paying a ferryman to set them on their way. As the need for public ferries increased, the government stepped in to regulate a ferry system that would provide economical and reliable travel. Both Virginia and Maryland passed laws, often similar albeit at different times, that regulated ferries.

The Virginia General Assembly passed an act in 1643 that established free ferries that ran from sunrise to sunset, funded by the county levy.[1] Evidently a clamor arose, for in four short years the assembly repealed the act as being a hardship on the poor who paid the tax yet did not travel. From then on county courts could establish ferries and their operating conditions, but the counties did not have to pay maintenance. Maintenance was paid by the person running the ferry. Virginia tried again in 1673 to establish a ferry act but was unsuccessful. More orderly acts were passed in the eighteenth century.

In 1702, the Virginia Assembly again enacted a law for public expresses and transportation of troops that did bring law and order to ferry travel. All ferries would be licensed by the court, run from sun-

A detail of Ogilby's Map of Maryland, 1671, showing the Chesapeake Bay.

rise to sunset, and charge only designated fees. Unlicensed boat owners who operated a ferry in the vicinity of a licensed one would be fined five pounds sterling unless they were transporting churchgoers. Perks of the job were as important then as now. A 1705 addition to the act stipulated that a keeper of a ferry give a ten-pound bond. He or she could own a tavern if there was not another one within five miles. If the ferryman neglected the work, his license would be revoked. No other ferry was to be established nearby. Anyone who did so would be fined. The violator paid the five-pound fine, of which half went to the county and the other half to the informer. As in the seventeenth-century acts, licensed ferrymen were exempt from paying public levies, serving in the militia, clearing highways, and impressment. They put the ferry at the disposal of the militia when necessary and the county would pay their ferriage as well as that of the official mail carrier, sheriffs, and officers. In 1712 the assembly deemed this act perpetual. Acts from 1720 onward addressed the matter of legal charges, including those for foot, horse, coach, wagon, and chaise traffic. The rates fluctuated and often fell as the number of travelers increased.

The growth of the major port towns, established primarily in the last decade of the seventeenth century, was caused by an increase in industry and resulted in improved roads. Portsmouth, Virginia became a shipbuilding center and, with nearby Gosport, produced naval stores and equipment. Norfolk had a rope walk and ship repair yard, but its dominant industry was its busy port. Alexandria became an important trading port particularly for wheat. Baltimore, which was not declared a town until 1729, later rivaled Norfolk as a trading port and center of shipyards and shipbuilding. Williamsburg and Annapolis relied on government with all its related businesses—attorneys, scriveners, tavern-keepers—as the base of their economy. Established travel routes between the burgeoning port towns required a multitude of ferries, one at least every fifteen miles and often every three miles.

Taking the ferry was as commonplace for the seventeenth- and eighteenth-century traveler as speeding across a bridge for the twenty-first century commuter, yet today there is scarcely a trace of the hundreds of sail or steam ferries that dotted the Chesapeake landscape. Reminders can be found on roadside historical markers, in place names such as Ferry Farm or Three Notch Road, or in the oral histories of tidewater residents. Written records of these enterprises are often incomplete,

This detail of Griffith's Map of Maryland, 1794, shows the transformation of the bay area through increased settlement and development.

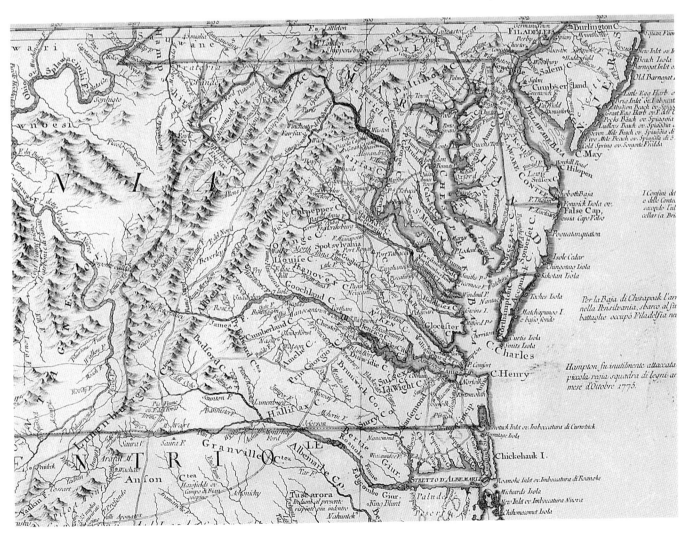

Virginia Pilot Boats.

The boat from which all these views were drawn was 58 feet upon the deck & drew 6 feet of water.—

B.H. Latrobe del.
March 7th 1796

Watercolor rendering of pilot boats in Virginia, 1796. These boats were used to ferry pilots from land to ships approaching the shore.

obscure, or inconclusive, yet remnants exist and offer insights into this complex transportation network. The Northern Neck of Virginia, where 98 percent of the land is within five miles of tidewater, gives an example of this proliferation. Prior to the Revolutionary War, as many as seven ferries operated across the Potomac River from King George County, Virginia to Charles County, Maryland.[2] Since these ferries often vied for the same crossing, there was constant rivalry among the ferrymen and some crossings survived for less than ten years. Virginia's licensing of ferries was intended to eliminate such rivalry.

Licensing aside, ferrying depended on the skill of the operator and the condition of the weather. Diarists often commented on the vagaries of each. In 1736, George Campbell, traveling from Virginia's Eastern Shore across the lower bay, stated that the shallop he was to sail in was anchored a mile from the Virginia shore due to a shoal and shallow water. Passengers got into a punt that Campbell stated was manned by oarsmen with paddles. The side of the punt was rammed by two cavorting porpoises, overturning it on the shoal. Campbell called the porpoises "stupid hogs."[3]

Ferrying could be a lucrative business. Entrepreneurs sought licenses for a specific spot and often obtained long-standing monopolies. On Virginia's Eastern Shore the Eyre family and their successors, the Bowdoin family, maintained a ferry from Hungar's Creek across the bay to Norfolk, Yorktown, and Hampton from 1745 to 1824. Littleton Eyre received the license for the ferry in 1745, ten years later had a ferry monopoly for Northampton County, and by 1767 for Accomack County as well. Ferry records of three months, from November 13, 1766, to February 27, 1767, show that Eyre and Bowdoin made twenty trips and carried fifty-two people, seventeen horses, one chariot, and some letters.[4] The Eyres and Bowdoins fought off one petitioner after another who endeavored to establish rival ferries. Some cases went as far as appellate court, but the courts upheld Eyre's and Bowdoin's exclusive licenses. During the Revolutionary War, the Bowdoins attempted a bit of war profiteering. The general assembly granted them the right to raise their rate to six pounds per crossing for one person in 1778 and twenty pounds the following year. As there was little or no journeying to war-ravaged Norfolk, one wonders if they profited at all. The Bowdoin's monopoly was broken in 1822 when John K. Floyd, who had received a license to run a ferry from King's Creek to Yorktown, Hampton, and Norfolk, purchased their ferry.[5]

In 1830, the Maryland and Virginia Steam Boat Company began a weekly packet trip from Norfolk to Cherrystone Wharf on Virginia's Eastern Shore. These sailing packets, forerunners of steamboats, operated on a regular schedule and carried freight and passengers from town to town. These were not daily round-trips, but usually left one town for another on one day and made the return trip a few days later.

Packet ownership changed frequently. In an effort to increase business, new owners often ran excursion boats that carried people to the Eastern Shore for a day of relaxation and "frequent refreshing." Between 1824 and 1840 four new packets began operation. The steamers took over even though the sailing sloops and schooners used for packets were advertised as copper-bottomed and fast.

It was, of course, the invention of the steamboat that wrought large changes in modes of ferry travel. James Rumsey, a native of Cecil County, Maryland, successfully demonstrated steamboating in 1787 when his motor-powered skiff made almost four knots on a trial run on the upper Potomac River. Three years later John Fitch launched his model. The side-wheeler *Clermont*, the result of collaboration between Robert Livingston and Robert Fulton, was launched in 1807 and is generally thought of as the "first steamboat."

Ultimately, steam and motors changed ferrying and made this mode of travel faster as well as more accommodating with the use of larger boats. Transportation of people and freight increased and conveyances never dreamed of by the sailing ferryman plied across from Virginia's Eastern Shore to the Hampton Roads area. Barges carried railroad freight cars, ferrying them across the bay; automobiles were ferried on motorized boats. Service for passengers and automobiles ceased in 1964 when the Chesapeake Bay Bridge Tunnel opened. The bridge tunnel linked the separated parts of Virginia and thus eliminated the need for cross-bay ferryboats.

CHAPTER 3

Potomac River Ferries

*"A ready Passage in most
Kinds of Weather"*

By the middle of the eighteenth century the growth
of major port towns resulted in frequently used travel routes. Travelers journeyed from the mouth of the bay via schooner ferry to the
Eastern Shore or across the James and York Rivers to the capital, Williamsburg. Additional routes developed from the head of the bay, leading the traveler south to Baltimore, Annapolis, and Williamsburg, or
north to Philadelphia—a destination of increasing importance as the
colonists pursued independence. Established ferries navigated these
river and bay crossings, often referred to in sojourners' diaries. Some
of the present-day automobile routes—for example, U.S. Route 1 and
Maryland Route 301—closely parallel the eighteenth-century roads.

By mid-century there was some improvement in the condition of
roads. Formerly muddy bogs in winter and dusty thoroughfares in
summer now stretched over sand or oyster shell bases on the eastern
side of the bay. Elsewhere, workers filled holes and ruts with brush
and logs. In many places deep ruts scarred the roads and proved perilous to stagecoach drivers and passengers. Near the end of the century, a traveler going from Elkton, Maryland, to Lower Ferry on the
Susquehanna River stated that the road was so often impassable that
the coach driver exhorted his passengers with the phrase, "Now gen-

tlemen to the left," or "Now gentlemen to the right," imploring them again and again to lean to one side to keep the vehicle on an even keel.

During his presidency, George Washington took two lengthy tours of the new country, honoring his pledge to visit all the states of the union. The first was in June 1789—a month-long tour of New England—and the second was a southern tour covering nearly two thousand miles in the spring of 1791. Travelling in his carriage from New York to Savannah, he was plagued by the bad state of the new republic's road system. On one ferry crossing his barge ran aground; on another his coach horse left the ferry before the boat reached shore. One contemporary hoped that the trip would "induce the Overseers of Roads and Ferry-Keepers to mend their ways and repair or build new boats."[1] Travel remained uncomfortable and uncertain well into the next century.

The ferries that crossed the Potomac, a major Chesapeake estuary, served as important links between these well-traveled roads. Popular translations for the Powhatan word "Patawomack" are "where one comes in," or "where it is brought in."[2] The Potomac begins its journey southeast of Cumberland, Maryland, continues its freshwater journey to the fall line above Georgetown, and then travels 120 tidal miles to the bay. Ferry operators plied this river from colonial times. Two of the main crossings were from Alexandria, Virginia and from Mathias Point, Virginia, to Cedar Point, Maryland.

Ferrymen were businessmen who aimed to succeed. Their newspaper advertisements emphasized good boats, skillful hands, and reasonable rates in addition to good entertainment, kind usage, crossing in all sorts of weather, and satisfaction guaranteed. The latter must have prevailed. Writing in 1765, the British traveler Lord Adam Gordon had nothing but praise for the ferries that, he said, speeded up travel in the colonies rather than slowing it as in other countries. Gordon added that the ferrymen assisted all strangers.

It was a boon to the traveler when a road led to a well-known ferry and its nearby ordinary. Ferrymen were the "Travelers' Aid Societies" of the day. They gave advice on the best and shortest travel routes, predicted the weather, held letters or parcels for one's arrival, passed on the latest gossip, and as the colonies got closer and closer to a rift with England, passed on the latest political news. Hooe's Ferry, which crossed the Potomac River from Mathias Point in King George County, Virginia, to Lower Cedar Point in Charles County, Maryland was one such place. The Hooes were descended from one of Virginia's earliest families. In the late 1690s, Rice Hooe received a patent for acreage in Stafford County (now King George County), Virginia. The land was

This view of Glatz's Ferry in Pennsylvania shows two ferries transporting stagecoaches and horses.

in an area known as Chotank that stretched as far north as Occoquan Creek and contained important plantations. In 1720, Rice Hooe received a license from the assembly to operate a ferry across the broad Potomac and charged two shillings per man or horse. Families in the Chotank neighborhood, noted for their hospitality, made frequent use of the ferry to visit relations and friends in the upper or lower Potomac settlements. Travelers also noted the Hooes' hospitality. Their large brick ferry house, which became a tavern, served as a haven for people being detained from crossing the water due to the weather or the time of day. The Hooes provided food, lodging, provender for horses, and comments on the latest news with gusto and largesse. On a moonlit night in mid-October 1765, Hooe detained a Scottish traveler who had endured "hot and sultry riding." The visitor stayed the night and later wrote that he got a cold dinner and more kindness than he guessed was shown to strangers in seven years. In another account, Richard Henry Lee wrote to South Carolinian Henry Laurens in 1779 inviting him to visit Chantilly, his Westmoreland County plantation, on his way south from New York. Lee told Laurens that his way

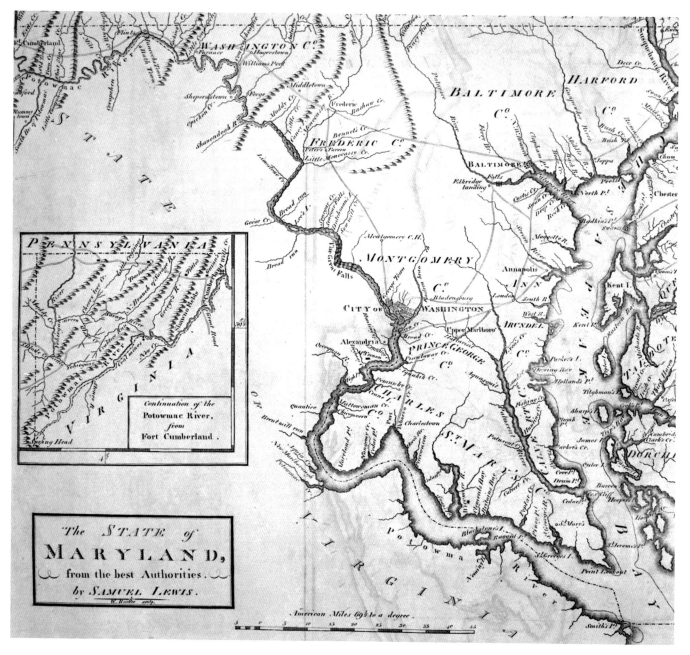

Samuel Lewis's map of Maryland, 1795, traces the route of the Potomac from the Chesapeake Bay in the south to western Maryland in the north.

was through Baltimore and across the Potomac at Hooe's and that the ferryman would give him directions.[3]

As Williamsburg and Annapolis grew in political importance, Hooe's became a vital link on the well-traveled north-south route between the two capitals and maintained its importance after 1779 as a transportation link between Richmond and Annapolis. George Washington referred in his diary to using it many times—in his chaise, or with his wife Martha and step-daughter Patsy Custis in the Mt. Vernon carriage on their way to Williamsburg or the Custis plantations. The road south from Alexandria, Virginia, the Old Potomac Path, wound through swampy land that was often impassable. To avoid this "mud and heavy going," Washington used the ferry run by John Posey to cross the Potomac to Thomas Marshall's Maryland land and then south to Hooe's, or to Port Tobacco where he again crossed the river and continued his journey south. John Thornton Posey was Washington's friend and neighbor, but he was an improvident man. He had bought two hundred acres on Dogue Run at the southwest corner of Mount Vernon from Washington's youngest brother, Charles. Posey later added six more acres, and in 1753 obtained a license to run a ferry from this spot now known as Ferry Point. Posey bought many other things to furnish his farm and home and borrowed to cover his expenditures. Washington lent him money and posted bond for him, but Posey could not repay his debts and may have lost control of the ferry. An advertisement in the *Maryland Gazette* in the fall of 1770 states:

> The Ferry lately kept by Captain Posey (over Patowmack River) from his Landing, to the Plantation of Captain T. Hanson Marshall, in Charles County, is still continued, and Travellers may depend upon a ready Passage in most Kinds of Weather, as there are good Boats of different Sizes, and strong Hands always attending."

In 1772, Washington acquired the ferry for fifty pounds in payment for Posey's bad debts and later advertised in the *Pennsylvania Gazette* that it could be rented. The business was "very pleasantly situated on the Patawmack River . . . a well accustomed Ferry, upon the most direct road leading from Annapolis through . . . Dumfries, and Fredericksburg to Williamsburg."[4] In 1790, Washington petitioned the general assembly to have the unprofitable ferry discontinued, and the legislators granted his request.

The Hooes, whose ferry business remained profitable, used small, open boats, probably shallops or sloops. Isaac Weld Jr., an Irishman who traveled in America from 1795 to 1797 and had very little good to say about the experience, noted in 1795 that winds had whipped up high waves on the three-mile crossing, and it was necessary to tie the horses. Tying the horses' legs together was a common practice if the weather was foul, as it kept them from overturning the boat with frightened kicks.[5]

In March 1764, John Laidler advertised in the *Maryland Gazette* that he had a good new yawl and could carry "Ladies and Gentlemen" from his landing (two miles above Lower Cedar Point) to Captain Hooe's in fifteen minutes. Laidler's (Laidlaws) was one of the Maryland landings used by Hooe's Ferry (which also used landings at Popes Creek, Port

Tobacco, and Nanjemoy). Various unlicensed ferries sailed from these same landings. One of them was run by a Mrs. Young, who lost her boats in 1776. Mr. Hooe then advertised in the August 14, 1776 *Maryland Gazette* that he would send over any of his boats for passengers to Virginia. All they had to do was hoist the flag or make a smoke "at the usual place." Despite the competition at this Potomac River crossing, one of whom advertised having "two as fine boats as any in America," Hooe's Ferry remained popular and prevailed.

During the Civil War the Hooes were suspected of receiving coded messages from southern sympathizers on the Maryland side of the Potomac. Olivia Floyd of Rose Hill on the Maryland side would gallop to Laidler's Ferry at night with any news of Union forces. The information would then be "blinked" across the river to Hooe's Ferry and reported to the Confederate Army. Union forces used "invasion scows" to ferry forty men and two cannon across the Potomac by rowing, towing, or poling, and the Confederates wanted to know their whereabouts. The Hooes also assisted Confederates traveling south. As a result, in 1861, William Budd, captain of a U.S. gunboat, burned their tavern-home.[6] The ferry business prevailed, however, under steam and under vari-

Harper's Ferry, West Virginia takes its name from the ferry licensed by Robert Harper in 1734, above the junction of the Potomac and Shenandoah Rivers. This painting by an unknown artist shows the town in the mid-nineteenth century.

ous managements until 1895—175 years of carrying people across the wide Potomac at approximately the spot where the Governor Henry W. Nice Memorial Bridge and Route 301 cross it today.

In the late eighteenth century, the Hooes had decided to expand their profitable transportation service with a ferry over Occoquan Creek on the northern edge of the Chotank neighborhood, but they did not count on the opposition of an unfriendly neighbor. George Mason, large landowner, author of the Virginia Bill of Rights and the Virginia State Constitution, owned a ferry over Occoquan Creek that his family had established years earlier. Travelers along that route then went to Dumfries, Stafford Court House, Fredericksburg, and points south.

George Mason's mother, widowed when he was ten, carefully husbanded her resources in order to leave an estate for her three children. In 1737 she rented her plantation on the southern side of the river to John Mercer. Mercer kept the profits and remained nine years, but she kept the right to the ferry on the well-traveled route. Mason did his best politicking to get the Hooes' 1791 petition for a license postponed until all the signatures against it were received. His argument, which won the day, was that a new ferry was unnecessary and would produce "much injury and oppression" to the people. In fact Mason's ferry was such a sound business investment that he left it in his will to his youngest son, Thomas Mason, and his heirs forever. The will stated:

> . . . all my land upon lower side of Occoquan River . . . together with the right and benefit of keeping the ferry . . . Which has been vested in me and my ancestors from the first settlement of this part of the country and long before the land there was taken up or patented.[7]

Mason also operated a two-decked cable ferry from land he owned above Arlington, across the Potomac, to the Maryland shore at the point where Rock Creek enters the river. A licensed ferry since 1748, Mason was as interested in maintaining a monopoly with this ferry as with the one over the Occoquan. In October 1776, Robert Peters and Thomas Richardson, who had ferries on the Maryland side opposite Mason's, petitioned the Maryland General Assembly that Mason's tenant had threatened them with a suit if they landed in Virginia and took on passengers. In fact, Mason had one ferryman arrested. Peters and Richardson stressed the importance of ferries "now," e.g., during wartime. A ferry operated continually at this spot for over a century until a toll bridge replaced it. This was often the fate of a ferry route once bridge-building became feasible. In 1888 a free bridge crossed the Potomac at the site of Mason's ferry. This was the first time in 150 years that it did not cost money to cross the Potomac River at Rock Creek.

There were other ferry crossings on the upper Potomac, some of the most important being those that sailed from Alexandria to connect the Virginia and Maryland sides of the post road. Alexandria began as a few scattered houses, a tobacco warehouse, and a ferry on land granted to Margaret Brent in 1654. In 1748 leading businessmen received a charter to turn the hamlet, with its deep port, into a town. In July of the following year, lots were sold according to the platted gridiron plan. In less than thirty years the port town thrived on trade with West Indian and European merchants and, with a population of over three thousand, ranked as the second largest town in Virginia.

In 1744, Hugh West received a license to operate a ferry from his landing at the foot of Oronoco Street to Frazier's Point, the Oxon Hill, Maryland, land of the Addison family. West advertised his ferry service as one that connected the "rising city of Alexandria with the opposite shore." It proved to be a popular route, and in subsequent years various operators leased the ferry. They catered to local traffic and to long-distance travelers going from Alexandria to Marlborough, Maryland, and across the Patuxent River, at either Nottingham or Queen Anne, and then to Londontown, Annapolis, and points north. In 1782, one of the ferry's renters, John Clifford, opened a tavern, "Ferry House," at the landing. This was probably an astute move, as in 1791 Alexandria became part of the new capital, Washington, D.C. A cornerstone laid in Alexandria marked the southern boundary of the federal city. Ferry traffic undoubtedly increased. In 1810, the Addisons sold their property to Zachariah Berry, and he and his descendants ran or leased the ferry until the 1870s.

Other ferry crossings between Maryland and Alexandria accommodated the busy traffic going to and from market, and competition developed. The usual custom was for the operator on one side to bring back passengers from the other side without fee, but Alexandrians complained to the Virginia Assembly that Maryland operators were trying to establish monopolies and charging for all crossings, sometimes demanding three times more than the law allowed. They wanted a law passed that would curtail this sort of activity, yet nothing seems to have come of the matter.[7] As was the case with Mason's Ferry at Rock Creek, the two state jurisdictions did not come to any joint legal settlement.

Early ferries were flat-bottomed scows propelled by pole or rope, or small sloops with their tenders in case the landing was not close enough to shore. After the War of 1812 a number of these boats were

Steamships such as the **William Jenkins** *arrived on the Potomac in 1837.*

replaced by ones propelled by horse power. Boatmen used paddle wheels, with teams of horses that turned the paddles in the center of the boat.

Steamboats came into use early in the nineteenth century. The July 13, 1837, *Alexandria Gazette* reported that Thomas Berry's new steamboat *Union* burst her boiler at the wharf and exploded, killing three people and injuring more. In the 1840s, George Fox leased the ferry rights from the Berry family and ran the side-wheeler *Alice Fox*. In 1852 the *Columbia*, a double-ended steam ferry, ran between the District of Columbia and Alexandria. The boat operated until the early twentieth century, when it caught fire and burned at its pier.

Nevertheless, the ferry business declined through the nineteenth century. The long bridge across the Potomac River between Alexandria and Washington made travel quicker and more convenient. In the 1860s two sailors, Captains Griffin and Wheatley, took over the Fox-Berry Ferry. They ran a "foot ferry," for passengers only, that was sailed or rowed. They called their boat *Hard Times*. Perhaps the hard times were caused by the Civil War when the Potomac was used by both Union and Confederate armies to the detriment of civilian travelers. In March 1862, Major General George B. McClellan used the Alexandria waterfront to amass a flotilla to carry the Army of the Potomac down the Chesapeake Bay. He requisitioned all available boats, including ferryboats.

CHAPTER 4

Other Virginia Ferries

*"It is the most irksome piece of business
to cross the ferries in Virginia"*

Virginia's population center shifted when Richmond became the capital in 1780. Proud Williamsburg, no longer the scene of lavish social activity and political debate, settled into a slow, drowsy decay for more than a century until John D. Rockefeller rescued it in 1926. Rivers and creeks remained the highways of the tidewater region, and ferries continued to operate until the middle of the twentieth century when road infrastructure developed over the area. This was especially true in heavily populated Norfolk, where cross-harbor ferrying functioned as a lifeline that grew in scope as the population increased.

The citizens of Norfolk, Virginia had depended on local, cross-harbor ferrying since 1636, when Adam Thoroughgood began his service across the Elizabeth River. Fronting on the Elizabeth and Hampton Roads, and laced with small creeks and inlets, Norfolk seemed destined to be a maritime community. Her citizens ferried back and forth to Portsmouth, to Berkeley as the city expanded southward, and to Hampton. The ferrying was constant, and as steam and motor took over, higher numbers of commuters traveled by water. The ferries operate today under the aegis of Hampton Roads Transit. A modern-day poster of the Elizabeth River ferryboats depicts the evolution of

Watercolor landscape of the James River.

that still-popular mode of travel, from the rowed skiff of 1636 to the 150-passenger diesel paddle wheeler of 1985 taking passengers from Norfolk to Portsmouth. Until the tunnel connected the two towns in 1952, several boats operated at the same time and ferried commuters and others back and forth across the Elizabeth. Regular users became fond of certain ferries. One of the most popular in the 1870s was the "Nanny Ferry," a side-wheeler with lattice framework on the upper deck railings, officially named the *Manhasset*. Nannies sat on the upper deck for a bit of gossip while their charges dashed around the deck, safe from falling into the water.

Bridges and tunnels now cross the Elizabeth, but old ferries never die. Hampton Roads Transit operates the Elizabeth River Ferry for commuters who want to avoid rush-hour traffic jams and for tourists who want a nostalgic trip. The service is called "Park and Sail." Paddle-wheel ferries cross every thirty minutes from the waterside in Norfolk to Portsmouth's North and High Street Landing. One of the ferries is powered by natural gas, making for fuel efficiency and a cleaner river.

From earliest times, water also connected Norfolk to Old Point Comfort, Hampton, and Newport News. A network of ferrymen established service in the area that grew in tandem with the population. In 1796, Irish traveler Weld complained that not one in six of the ferries he used was good or well-manned: "It is the most irksome piece of business to cross the ferries in Virginia." Weld was irate because at the ferry crossing between Hampton and Norfolk he had to leave his horses behind until boarding flats, or ramps, could be found. He found Hampton to be a "dirty, disagreeable place, always infected by a shocking stench from a muddy shore when tide is out."[1] With its safe anchorage, boatmen had used Hampton since earliest times as a place to wait for a fair wind, and no doubt the marshes reflected the results of human activity.

Hampton Roads ferries ran from Newport News to Norfolk and from Old Point Comfort to Willoughby Spit. The new steamboat side-wheeler *Sea Horse* was built in 1812 and advertisements stated that the boat could carry horses and carriages between Norfolk and Hampton. Other similar vessels were added to the route, which had an informal schedule. Almost a century later, in 1901, the Norfolk and Atlantic Terminal Company operated these ferries on a frequent and regular schedule between Pine Beach in Norfolk to Old Point Comfort and to the railroad pier at Newport News. In 1907, the Jamestown Exposition caused a great spurt in the ferry business, as tourists had to be transported across Hampton Roads to the fairgrounds in Norfolk. A special pier was built at the end of Ivy Avenue in Newport News and trolley rails were placed to its end where passengers alighted and transferred to small boats.

In 1912, the Chesapeake Ferry Company was organized and began running double-ended ferries on a regular schedule across Hampton Roads. *Ocean View* ran hourly from Old Point Comfort to Willoughby Spit. The company added *Willoughby* and *Annie L. Vansciver* in the summer to accommodate the numerous sailors on liberty. They ferried to Willoughby and then rode a trolley into downtown Norfolk for a day or night on the town. By 1929 there were five large, double-ended ferries crisscrossing Hampton Roads. Four of them were side-wheelers, known by their passengers as "Walk in the Waters." On April 30, 1948, passengers aboard the screw-propelled *Ocean City* probably wished that the double-ended boat *could* walk on the water. On this memorable trip, the normal thirty-minute run took four hours as her drunken captain and mate wove back and forth across the Roads, narrowly missing boats of all sizes. They missed their berth and finally crashed to a halt into the pilings of an abandoned pier in the James River, much to the relief of many hysterical riders. The captain and mate each were fined ten dollars and lost their jobs.

The Virginia State Highway Commission gained control of the Chesapeake Ferry Company in 1946 when the ferry operators went out on strike. The commission scrapped the old paddle-wheelers and added more modern vessels. Finally, in 1957, the agency closed the entire system when the Hampton Roads Bridge-Tunnel complex opened, carrying more cars and passengers than old-time ferrymen could have imagined.

While the larger steam- and then motor-powered vessels ran in heavily populated areas, the rural parts of tidewater Virginia continued their dependence on small power-driven ferries. These were usually cable-driven scows that crossed creeks and rivers where well-traveled roads led to the water's edge, areas not bridged until the mid-twentieth century. As late as 1895 the general assembly responded to citizens' requests and approved establishment of the Great Wicomico Ferry and its route from Tiper's to Blackwell's Wharf in the Northern Neck of the state. The company built a forty-foot boat, with side railings and hinged aprons at either end, the same model that had plied the waters since the eighteenth century. Even the twelve-foot by fourteen-foot ferry house built for the ferryman reflected the past. The ferryman, on call at all times, lived on site. County residents traveled free of charge and all others paid ten cents a head per person, twenty-five cents for a horse and rider, or fifteen cents per cow.

In 1892, Oliver Christian obtained the license, for $100 per year, to run the ferry. He was paid quarterly by Northumberland County, but only received one-half pay the first and second quarters. The other half was retained as security for faithful performance of duties. Ferrymen moved on every year or so, and the pay fluctuated with the changes. In 1901, L. E. Headley was given $60 in addition to his stipend to cover the cost of building a new boat. He then lost a month's salary because the ferry did not run while the boat was being built. In December 1928 the licensed ferrymen were terminated as the State Highway Commission took over the service. The state ran it until the Tiper's Bridge opened about eight years later.

By the year 2000 the state was still in the ferry business. The Department of Transportation ran the Jamestown Ferry, the Sunnybank Ferry, and the Merry Point Ferry. The Jamestown Ferry crosses the James River between Jamestown and Scotland, a fifteen-minute trip that takes automobile passengers from the historic area of Williamsburg-Jamestown, bustling with tourists, to quiet, rural, historic Surry County. The large diesel-powered *Pocahontas*, *Williamsburg*, *Surry*, and *Virginia*, crisscross the river twenty-four hours a day. In 1925, Captain Albert M. Jester launched the *Captain John Smith*, the area's first automobile ferry. The state took over the operation in 1945. Today, resident or not, there is no charge for using the Jamestown Ferry.

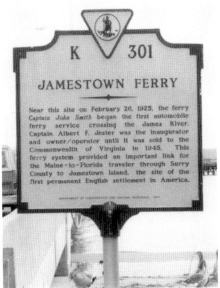

Scenes from a trip on the Jamestown Ferry, including a sign to let riders know a little about the ferry's history.

On March 14, 1906, the Board of Supervisors of Northumberland County approved establishing a public ferry across the Little Wicomico River in response to a citizen petition that stressed the need for a crossing between Hack's Neck and Sunnybank. Ferry service cut the commuter distance by two-thirds for the men employed by the menhaden fishing industry. A wooden cable ferry propelled by a notched stick was put in use, and the ferryman's job went to the lowest bidder for twenty-eight to thirty dollars a month. By 1910 a motorboat went into service, and the ferryman got thirty dollars a month, tips, and all the money charged for cars not from Northumberland County. The next ferryman was once admonished by the county board of supervisors for not operating in a businesslike manner. The complaint against him was that he did not answer bells properly, and did not open the ferry at sunrise, sometimes being as late as 9:00 A.M., too late for school children.[2] But generally he must have served well, for he kept the position for twenty-five years.

The ferry Pocahontas, *part of the Jamestown Ferry service, departs in a cloud of smoke.*

The Sunnybank Ferry.

In 1932 the Department of Highways took over the Sunnybank Ferry and improved the roads, and thus ended the era in which cars had to be pushed or pulled through sand going onto and coming off the ferry. Commuters and tourists continue to use this service. It is still a cable-powered scow with one modern innovation, a canvas half-roof that wards off the hot sun. The boat can hold three small or two large cars, is hailed by blowing one's car horn, and is free for all travelers from Sunnybank to Ophelia on Route 644, from sunrise to sunset every day of the week except Sunday.

The Merry Point Ferry, across the western branch of Virginia's Corrotoman River, in Lancaster County, was established by the county in 1847 and taken over by the state in 1932. A cable-driven, two-car ferry with a pilot's cabin, it is reached at the end of a narrow, winding, tree-shaded road off Route 604. A sign at the junction of the two roads notifies passengers whether the ferry is open or closed for the day. It is closed on Sundays, which is a reversal of eighteenth-century operating times, when carrying people to church was one of a ferry's main reasons for existence. The Merry Point Ferry runs from 7:00 a.m. until 7:00 p.m. the other days of the week.

CHAPTER 5

Development
of a Ferry System
in Maryland

"Every day as Passengers
Shall Requir"

The proprietors of seventeenth-century Maryland were as concerned about their colony's lack of town development as King Charles II had been for Virginia. In 1668, Governor Charles Calvert designated eleven sites suitable for sea ports. These sites included harbors or creeks where he felt maritime commerce would thrive. Four years later he listed fifteen desirable sites. The general assembly enacted legislation in 1683, 1684, and 1686 that designated fifty-three town sites along the water. Just as these town acts resembled those the Virginia lawmakers passed, ferrying in the Maryland colony closely followed its southern neighbor's development. The earliest ferries were dugout canoes or small rowed or poled boats run by individuals for personal convenience or for hire. As was the case in Virginia, it became apparent that the government should regulate transportation, and in 1658 the Maryland General Assembly passed a law that provided for a ferry for each county except Kent. The ferries ran at the county's expense and under the administration of the local courts. The courts appointed the ferry keepers, decided ferry locations, specified types of boats, and set operator fees. Anyone operating a rival ferry was subject to fine. On June 4, 1658, the assembly authorized one Samuel Harris to "keepe the ferre ouer Wicokomeko River" and ordered that "sayd

"The Founding of Maryland," as painted by Emanuel Leutze in 1861.

Samuel Harrise shal attend this ferrie from Sone Rising to Sone set."[1] This was the Wicomico River on the western side of the bay. Sunrise to sunset became the standard operating hours for future ferries. Harris earned two thousand pounds of tobacco yearly and the county agreed to furnish him with a boat. County lawmakers also agreed to pay Goodman Smote (Smoot) seven hundred pounds of tobacco for building the boat. Six years later Thomas Brandson was granted two thousand pounds of tobacco yearly to "twise a day to go over Wicohomico River wheather thear bee any occasion or No And as often every day as Passengers Shall Requir."[2] This was probably the same ferry.

Boats often changed hands and when they did went by the owner's name. For example, in the eighteenth century, Reubin Perkins bought the ferry Thomas Cresap established across the Susquehanna River in 1733. The business became Perkins' Ferry, Smith's Ferry in 1772, and Bell's Ferry in 1793. This changing of names can make it difficult to locate the exact route of a ferry. Further confusion arises from the fact that some geographical names used in early descriptions, such as

King's Creek, no longer exist on maps. Crossing as often as a passenger required was another stipulation written into future laws.

In the early years passengers paid ferrymen in the currency of the time, pounds of tobacco, the staple commodity. European demand for Chesapeake tobacco had steadily increased from the time John Rolfe sent the first shipment to England in 1613. Coins were scarce, and tobacco became the "money," yet its value varied by seasonal quality and by curing methods. As a perishable commodity it was difficult to transport or handle, and was held in warehouses until it could be shipped across the Atlantic Ocean. In 1753, the Maryland legislators passed an act to establish public warehouses where tobacco could be stored and inspected.[3] Many of these warehouses were located at well-used ferries, and the ferrymen were appointed to be inspectors. The governor appointed individuals that vestrymen and church wardens recommended. The chosen ferrymen were good businessmen and men of good standing in their communities. The ferryman at the Nanticoke River on Maryland's Eastern Shore received twenty-five pounds of tobacco to inspect the hogsheads at the warehouse above Crather's Ferry. John Holland at Bohemia Ferry received the same amount, while Henry Enalls Jr. at the Choptank Ferry received fifty pounds. Although by the mid-eighteenth century paper money and other commodities were replacing tobacco as currency, the county courts still paid ferrymen in tobacco. More than a century after the appointments of Samuel Harris and Thomas Brandson, Maryland's Worcester County Levy showed a yearly stipend of 2,500 pounds of tobacco to Mary Stevens for operating the lower ferry over the Pocomoke River on Maryland's

The Pocomoke River, where Mary Stevens plied her trade.

Eastern Shore. Similarly, the Cannon family earned 1,500 pounds of tobacco for keeping their ferry over the Nanticoke River. The counties still retained control and tobacco was still the currency.

It is interesting to note that today Cannon's ferry still operates across the Nanticoke River as the Woodland Ferry. The Woodland Ferry, which crosses the tidal Nanticoke River in what is now Sussex County, Delaware, boasts a unique ferry adjunct: the Woodland Ferry Association, which received a grant of ten thousand dollars from the state of Delaware. The group used part of the money for an eye-catching brochure full of color pictures and historical information. Other expendi-

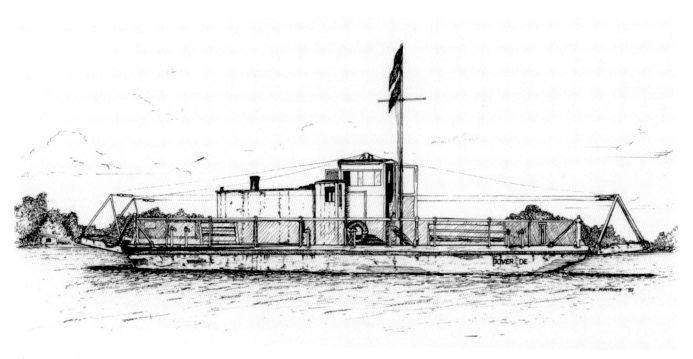

The sketch of the Woodland Ferry above is by Chris Matthes. The photo shows the ferry at the dock, with the Cannon House on the opposite shore.

The Severn River at sunset, in an oil painting from 1848.

tures included the Woodland Ferry Park, an informal garden spot near the ferry ramp on the Woodland side. The association also organized two annual get-togethers for ferry enthusiasts, the Woodland Ferry Festival and the Open Golf Tournament, both held in September.

In 1793, Elizabeth and Isaac Cannon received a fourteen-year license to operate the ferry.[4] The ferry's location, on the main north-south road with service across the Nanticoke, ensured its prosperity. In time, U.S. Route 13 became the main road between Seaford and Laurel, Delaware, and the ferry now connects Road 78. The Cannon Ferry, as it was originally known, remained in the family with sons Jacob and Isaac taking over the business. Unscrupulous businessmen, the Cannons took over everything through usury and forfeiture, and established their own small kingdom with warehouses, a sailing fleet, and over 4,500 acres of farmland, stores, rental tenant houses, and slaves. They became money lenders, hated because they showed no leniency. In one case they took a stew pot off the hob for payment of a debt. In 1820, Jacob built two-story, five-bay Cannon Hall for his intended bride. The lady jilted him, however, and he never lived in the house. Privately owned today, it is open during the Woodland Festival. In 1843, Jacob disputed Owen O'Day's right to a bee tree, claiming it was on his property, and charging O'Day eighteen dollars. Infuriated, O'Day met him at the wharf and shot him. Doctors called to the scene could not save Jacob. Isaac died a month after Jacob's death.

During this turbulent period the ferry also was used by Patty Cannon, another unscrupulous dealer who captured free blacks, imprisoned them in attics and sheds, and sold them to slavers at the ferry wharf. She netted as much as $1,000 per person and ran her business for forty years until the law finally caught up with her. She committed suicide in jail.[5]

The bustling town gradually quieted and its name was changed to Woodland. Woodland Ferry, a steel cable ferry licensed by the U.S. Coast Guard, is operated daily by the state of Delaware. Like ferries from the beginning, its service can be curtailed by ice or freezing rain. Recently, the Woodland Ferry service was ended and the old ferryboat put up for auction. A new vessel was christened and entered service October 29, 2008.

The Maryland General Assembly repealed the 1658 act regulating ferries and the colony developed a system different from that of Virginia. County courts licensed ferries that carried any traveler free of charge. Private ferries could operate without restraint or license. The private operator ran his business wherever traffic warranted, charged whatever the traffic would bear, set his own hours of business, and

Burkhalter's Ferry on the Susquehanna River, in a watercolor drawing.

decided whether he would carry horses, cattle, and vehicles as well as people. This dual system caused confusion. As early as 1681, Joseph Norwood of Anne Arundel County humbly petitioned the court for a license to do what he had been doing, ferrying people across the Severn River. As late as 1788, Lawson Speaks of Charles County was fined five pounds for keeping a ferry without a license. He stated in his brief that he had made application, received a verbal nod, and was too lame to get to the county court to purchase the license. In other cases new ferry operators pleaded ignorance of the license law. One such person asked that the fine be remitted because he had a large family and could barely support them. The court granted his request.[6]

This dual system of government-licensed and privately operated ferries continued, but the system chafed Charles Calvert, Lord Baltimore, who maintained it was his proprietary right to regulate all ferries and thus receive the license revenue. In 1734, Calvert informed Lieutenant Governor Samuel Ogle that all ferries were to be licensed for a three-year period and that anyone setting up a ferry on their own could be "Discountenanced by all the Magistrates of the Province." Many objected. For example, Baltimore County justices were loath to relinquish their right to levy taxes to support a ferry system and maintained that such had been the practice for a long time. The officials drafted and approved a petition in which they stated that they had a lawful right to operate a ferry over the Patapsco River. In 1741, a people's committee representing those who maintained their right to operate private ferries petitioned the assembly. They believed the proprietor's agents prevented "Necessary Boats and convenient Vessels from transporting and carrying over such Bays Rivers Creeks and Inletts his Majestys Subjects to the great delay and hindrance of Business Publick and Private."[7] A 1742 bill to regulate the ferries came to naught, and Lord Baltimore lost his bid for a licensing monopoly. This pleased Governor Horatio Sharpe, who had long favored county control. By 1764, ferry systems had spread throughout the colony, and Sharpe could announce that ferries—with a ferryman in constant attendance—had been established over every river crossed by a road. This resulted in publicly administered and privately run ferries operating in competition with one another throughout tidewater Maryland. The ferries paid for by county levy were to adhere to special requirements, such as time of operation, the number of attendants for each boat, the number of horses to be carried, whether wheat and other produce should be transported, and free passage for churchgoers on Sundays.

Irregular travel on a ferry route proved to be expensive. The county paid to keep the man and boat operating from sunup to sundown, and no method to oversee a ferryman's compliance with the law existed. Consequently, disgruntled citizens reported breaches of service, such as charging more than the set fare (the informer received half the fine). For example, in April 1786, Reuben McDaniel deposed that Samuel Iiams was absent from his ferry over the South River near Londontown until 10:00 A.M. Iiams pleaded to the assembly that he had provided unremitting satisfaction for several years and that at the time referred to he was only a short distance away gathering wood. When Iiams added that he would not leave the ferry for any other purpose, the court ordered that he pay a minimal fine.[8] Operators who left ferries unattended faced serious consequences. In more than one case, owners left slaves to operate the ferry. Concerned citizens charged mismanagement and asked the court for the operator's removal.[9] Newspaper advertisements often included the words "always manned"—what good was a ferry without a ferryman?

Advertisements that boasted "always manned" did not specify the ferryman's qualifications. In an era devoid of channel markers and local charts, it was imperative that an operator know his way. When he did not, chaos resulted. In March 1791, George Washington, a frequent traveler, fumed at the "unskillfulness of hands" during a trip across Chesapeake Bay. Washington was on his way from Philadelphia to Mount Vernon by way of Rock Hall, Maryland, where he caught the ferry for Annapolis. He had left Philadelphia on the morning of March 21, spent the night at Chester, Pennsylvania, the next night at New Castle, Delaware, and the last night at Chestertown, Maryland. In the morning Washington rode to Rock Hall where there was a delay in procuring the four boats his entourage needed. Washington was traveling with his chariot, horses, and servants. He had traveled this way before, the crossing taking two and a half to three hours, and was therefore not concerned when they were not able to depart until mid-afternoon. Shortly, a light wind and calm caused a further delay. As they entered the mouth of the Severn River, Washington wrote:

> the ignorance of the People on board, with respect to the navigation of it run us a ground first on Greenbury point from whence with much exertion and difficulty we got off; and then, having no knowledge of the Channel and the night being immensely dark with heavy and variable squalls of wind, constant lightning and tremendous thunder, we soon got aground again on what is called Horne's point.[10]

After spending a miserable night on board, the group arrived in Annapolis the next day and Washington never again traveled across the bay. The president took the northern route across the mouth of the Susquehanna River whenever he traveled from Mount Vernon to Philadelphia.

Washington's diary is full of listings of ferries or ferriage, and he sometimes noted that he had paid the cost of the trip. Other entries listed settlements of running bills and reflected his regular use of particular ferries. For example, the entry for October 22, 1772, states "By year's & 3 Months Ferriage at ye lower Ferry on Rappahannock opposite my Mothers. 12s 6d."[11] Washington often rode this way to attend the assembly in Williamsburg or to inspect his holdings on the Northern Neck, Ferry Farm, and Custis estates.

Aside from hazards caused by inept ferrymen, travelers also were subject to delays, accidents, and even death by fiercely capricious weather, which in the tidewater often came up suddenly. In the fall of 1769, the *Maryland Gazette* reported that people impatient to attend the races in Annapolis packed the ferry over the Severn River. A wind was "blowing fresh" and the overcrowded boat went down within two hundred yards of shore, "by which unhappy Accident" Mr. Samuel Marlow and another man were drowned. The *Gazette* went on to report that the horses and other passengers were saved with "utmost difficulty." In 1793, one Thomas Castin was ferrying across the Chesapeake Bay toward Baltimore when the "Boate Over Sett." Eight people drowned and others saved themselves by clinging to the mast until rescued two hours later by the ferry from Rock Hall.[12]

A calm could be just as disturbing. When crossing the Delaware River in May 1774, on his way from Princeton, New Jersey, to Nomini Hall on Virginia's Northern Neck, Philip Vickers Fithian had to help the ferryman at Port Penn. He took "to the Oar and pull[ed] like a Turk" for over an hour. They finally reached shore a mile above the usual ferry landing. Fithian then rode over unfamiliar land in the dark of night to the tavern, where he ordered a gill of bitters to "qualify my humours" and a dish of tea to "cheer me." Fithian encountered trouble at the Port Penn ferry just once, yet after his last trip, in October 1774, he wrote that he arrived home by "God's kindness."[13]

Travelers often suffered delays. If a passenger arrived at a ferry just as the sun was setting he often had to wait until the next morning—even on a moonlit night few operators would chance a crossing. Very low tides or heavy fog could cause delay. Severe winter weather with ice, snow, and storms brought ferrying to a standstill, and at times passengers voted to try to push the boat through an icy river. If the ice was six or seven inches thick, as it was on the Chesapeake Bay in 1780, the passengers simply rode or drove their carriages across. In

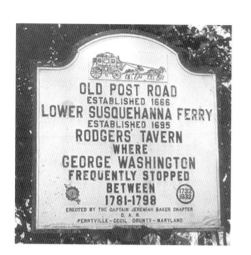

A sign commemorating the Lower Susquehanna Ferry and Rodgers Tavern, noting the George Wahington connection.

1808, Benjamin Henry Latrobe wrote to Thomas Jefferson that he was delayed for three days trying to cross the Susquehanna River at Columbia, Pennsylvania, because of ice on the opposite shore.

Waiting overnight or waiting for days, passengers needed a place to stay. Affluent travelers were always welcomed at the homes of nearby friends or relatives and could look forward to an evening of good food, good company, and comfortable repose. Otherwise they took their chances with fellow travelers at the ferry house and often wrote of how they fared at the ordinary. Every major ferry kept an ordinary—so-called because it served "ordinary" food and drink—and by 1746 there were 845 licensed establishments in the Maryland colony. The general assembly enacted liquor license laws by 1666 under the jurisdiction of the county courts, which set the prices that could be charged for spirits. In 1668, Virginia enacted a law limiting one "small tippling" house to a ferry. It was the tippling that was most profitable for the tavern keeper and the tippling that was regulated by law. A 1780 Maryland act specified that spirits could be sold "only by sealed measures, except bottled cider, perry, quince drink, and strong beer of the produce of this state, and such liquors as shall come into this State in bottles." The law also specified that an ordinary not at a court house must provide three beds with coverings, a stable large enough for at least six horses, and food for the same.[14]

Diarists wrote about their experiences at the ferry house. Philip Vickers Fithian noted that he spent Friday night April 17, 1774, at Port Tobacco, then the capital of Charles County, Maryland, and an important port. It was a frequent stopover for travelers going to and from Philadelphia. A traveler would expect to find good lodging at Port Tobacco, but Fithian wrote that all night long he had the company of bugs in every part of his bed and could hear noisy fellows in the next room playing billiards.[15] At other times in his travels he found friendlier hosts and wrote of receiving gallons of corn and oats for his horse and a bowl of punch and food for himself, giving the ferryman a bottle of rum, and having a barber to shave and dress him.

Accommodations varied, of course, from ferry house to ferry house, but the owners all touted them in various advertisements in local newspapers. Those placed in the *Maryland Gazette* often included the words "Good beds, pasturage and lodging (for horses) gratis, liquor and provider."

Two Europeans commented on their ferry house experience. Isaac Weld Jr. found a tavern so much to his liking that he wrote there was a bright fireside and good dinner. Weld added that thirteen travelers who spent the night included lawyers, a judge, and some boorish farmers. As was often the case, all sorts of people bedded together, but

Rodgers Tavern as it looks today.

Weld and a friend thanked their lucky stars that they got the second bedroom in the house.[16] In 1800, John Davis, an inveterate traveler from Salisbury, England, wrote that he had elegant accommodations at a tavern on the banks of the Susquehanna River, including a mulatto girl to brush away flies with a peacock feather while they were dining.[17] Weld and Davis probably were referring to Rodgers Tavern, a well-known hostelry on the eastern side of the much-used Susquehanna Lower Ferry. The building is extant.

Fortunately for the historical record, other men kept diaries regarding the use of ferries. In the first half of the nineteenth century, one John Blackford kept a ferry over the Potomac between Sharpsburg, Maryland, and Shepherdstown, Virginia (now West Virginia). His diary, with its daily notations, is a picture of the business during the 1830s. Blackford hired hands to run his ferry, usually having two or three working together. Time and time again he commented that one of them, Julius, (is) "in the ferry boat drunk as he usually is when

there." Once when Julius was away all day Blackford whacked him with a broom. Blackford checked the ferriage receipts regularly and noted the day's take: "done a good business . . . little doing at the ferry . . . moderate business . . . tolerable good business . . . verry poor business." In August 1830 a nearby Methodist camp meeting gave a great boost to business. In January 1831 he had all hands cutting ice to make a channel for the ferry. His comments on unreliable help, weather hazards, and fluctuating business could be applied to any operation.[18]

Today, a much-used commuter ferry operates across the Potomac near Poolesville, Maryland. Now known as White's Ferry, it was the scene of intense skirmishing during the Civil War. In 1828, Ernest Conrad had established a poled ferry that came to be known as Conrad's Ferry. Conrad had a grain warehouse on the Virginia side of his enterprise and a post office named for him on the Maryland side. The ferry was an important shipping point, particularly after the Chesapeake and Ohio Canal, paralleling the Potomac River, was completed in 1850. The ferry's importance during the Civil War was due to its proximity to Washington, D.C. and its location in a thriving agricultural area.

Elijah Viers White of Poolesville was a southern sympathizer who in 1861 organized a troop of Marylanders into the Thirty-fifth Virginia Battalion and took his men across the Potomac on Conrad's Ferry. His knowledge of the terrain benefited his troops as they raided the area. In their last engagement, February 1865, the troops skirmished at Edwards' Ferry, south of Conrad's Ferry and opposite Leesburg, Virginia, against the First Delaware Cavalry in February 1865. On May 25, 1865, Elijah White (now Colonel) signed his oath of allegiance to the

United States and began a business career. He began first with a farm, then a fancy goods store, a fertilizer and grain business, and then with Conrad's Ferry, which he bought in 1871 and where he established warehouses. From then on it was known as White's Ferry. During the years the ferryboat went through the usual metamorphosis from rope cable to steel cable to gasoline-powered tug to wooden barge to steel barge with a jet engine to today's steel barge propelled by a diesel tug. The boat is named *Jubal A. Early* after the Confederate general who crossed there in July 1864 following his raid on Washington. The tug is dubbed "Early's Aid," a reminder that during the Civil War skirmishing there were southerners everywhere in the area.

CHAPTER 6

Middle Bay Ferry Crossings

"As good as 'any that cross the bay' "

Early settlers traveled by way of Indian paths, most of which cut through forests. If a traveler came to an obstacle such as a downed tree, he dealt with it as he saw fit, by going around it. The next traveler might go around it on the other side, thus making two paths. In some places five routes developed around an obstacle in the road, and few were marked with signs to direct the confused traveler. Early routes were also established with the rise of tobacco growing in the region. "Rolling roads" were established over which hogsheads of tobacco were rolled to the nearest wharf. Early roadways were also created when landowners built "woods roads" that led to the best stands of trees for firewood, essential both for cooking and warming the hearth.

In 1666, the Maryland General Assembly passed laws meant to foster travel. This first road legislation called "for making highwaies and making the heads of Rivers, Creeks, Branches and Swamps passable for horse & foote."[1] In September 1696, Maryland enacted additional road legislation. This new law called for substantial bridges over the heads of creeks and their branches where the county justices declared a need for the same. Legislators also called for roads to be cleared and grubbed to a width of twenty feet. Justices were to record the names

A hogshead barrel being pulled by a horse and an ox along a rolling road.

of those byways considered the "Publick Rhoades" and refer to the information in road alteration cases. Anyone charged with altering a public road faced a fine of five hundred pounds of tobacco, a stiff fine indeed.

A road's right-of-way might very well go through fenced private property. Gates into and out of the property had to be open and shut by the traveler. Tampering with the gates could constitute a clear case of altering a road. By 1704, Maryland's lawmakers called for both sides of a road to be marked with two notches on a tree if the road led to a ferry, courthouse, church, or the port of Annapolis. If the road to the ferry branched off from the main road, it was to be marked with three notches spaced equally apart.[2] Fundamental to colonial travel and essential for transportation, ferry landings and crossings warranted inclusion on the list of most important road markers.

As roads improved, well-used routes established links with favorite ferries. Among the most frequented on the north-south route from Philadelphia to Williamsburg were the ferries that crossed the Chesapeake Bay. The earliest of these cross-bay ferries began sailing from the safe haven of Broad Creek on Kent Island to Anne Arundel

County in the mid-seventeenth century. It is no wonder the service originated at that site—Virginia's William Claiborne had settled Kent Island and established a trading post before Calvert's settlers arrived at St. Mary's. Claiborne imported people, and a settlement that included a jail, courthouse, ordinary, and ferry soon followed.

The Maryland Assembly passed a bill in 1671 that established licensed ferries from Anne Arundel County to Kent Island. A hundred years later the island ferrymen advertised their businesses in the *Maryland Gazette* with enticements such as good boats and experienced hands, and a house of entertainment that "will please and give satisfaction to customers." In 1768, Sarah Flynn advertised such amenities. Women often became ferry keepers upon the death of their husbands and simply took over the businesses. Some renewed their licenses year after year and had the same protection of the law as their male counterparts. In 1710, Mrs. Ann Lyunes, widow of ferryman Philip Lyunes, petitioned the Maryland assembly after ferrymen damaged her corn and tobacco crops. The lawmakers granted her monopoly rights, but she could only charge the same ferriage as had her husband. In 1786, the Dorchester County Court granted Elizabeth Travers a license to operate her late husband Henry's ferry over Slaughter Creek. The license, per Maryland law, specified that she keep the ferry in good order, use a boat capable of carrying three horses at once, and employ two able-bodied ferrymen. The court also specified the amount she could charge for passengers and their horses and carriages. Paid $350 per year, Mary Selby and Mary Duvall operated ferries over the Severn River as late as 1832, years after they became widows.[3] Other widows rented out the ferries their husbands had once operated. Upon her husband's death, George Mason's mother rented her farm but retained the right to the ferry and its profits.

Most ferry operators were men—James Hutchings advised those who wished to use his ferry from Annapolis to Broad Creek to go to the Blue Ball Tavern to seek him out. Those who wished to use Samuel Middleton's Ferry went to his popular tavern on the Annapolis waterfront, where the Tuesday Club, the Jockey Club, and the Free Masons met. Middleton advertised that his green sailing boat, rigged schooner-fashion and decked as far as its stern, had a twenty-foot keel and was as good as "any that cross the bay, hopes to meet with encouragement."[4] Another ferry operator, Ashbury Sutton, proved his mettle in 1760 when an unexpected gust of wind overset his boat. He swam to shore to get another and thus saved his passengers. When winds were calm and skies blue, passengers enjoyed the scenery—wooded shores, porpoises and dolphins, wildfowl in season, and the many sloops and barks plying the bay.

Ferry rates did not change, from the time Ashbury Sutton advertised in 1746 until 1768 when Middleton listed the following, "man and horse 10s, single man 5s, chair 7s 6d." Middleton stayed in business until at least 1784, when Thomas Jefferson noted in his journal that he paid Middleton ten dollars for passage to Rock Hall and added that he gave the sailors 8/4 .[5] It is interesting to note that Thomas Jefferson paid the ferryman a sum separate from the ferriage. From the amount, it can be assumed that the payment was obligatory. George Washington occasionally listed payments in the same manner, but more often noted only the ferriage.

Advertisements in the early nineteenth century mention larger boats. In 1813, R. I. Jones stated that his large, fast-sailing sloop, *Caroline*, could convey passengers, horses, and carriages. Jones had received his license from the Queen Anne's County Levy Court in 1811, and he charged one dollar per person to cross the bay if he carried more than one passenger. The Broad Creek to Annapolis ferries ran as late as 1858 and advertised their location "on the main post-road."

The ferry across the Chesapeake from Rock Hall to Annapolis traveled a greater water distance than did the one at Broad Creek. Travelers who wanted a shorter land trip, however, favored the Rock Hall transport and noted the trip in their diaries.[6] They wrote of schooner-rigged boats either decked, half-decked, or open and large enough to carry man, horse, and carriage. If there was a delay due to weather, or for procurement of boats on the Rock Hall side, patrons could pass the time at the races. During one layover, Fithian commented that when his landlord took him to the nearby racecourse he was shocked to note that over a third of the attendees were in mourning.[7]

To illustrate how common and indispensable ferries were, consider the following journey. In 1775, Thomas Jefferson, on his way to a meeting of the Second Continental Congress in Philadelphia, left Williamsburg on June 11, crossed the Pamunky River on Ruffin's Ferry, ferried across the Rappahannock River on June 15, then crossed the Potomac at Hooe's Ferry, and the South River at Londontown on June 17. He used the ferry from Annapolis to Rock Hall the next day, paid 18/4 ferriage, and gave the ferryman 5/2½. His lodgings at Greentree's in Rock Hall cost 18/4. From Rock Hall he went on to Philadelphia.

On August 3, 1775, on his way home from Philadelphia, Jefferson took James Hodges' White Rock Hall Ferry. Hodges kept a ferry house and Jefferson paid him 1/8 above the cost of his "breakfast, ferriage, & etc." James Hodges was one of several entrepreneurs who ran ferries from Rock Hall. Abraham Ayres was another, and he advertised in the *Maryland Gazette* that his ferries, going to Annapolis or to Baltimore, were the best two-decked boats, with good hands and good entertain-

ment for man and horse. In a July 10, 1769, advertisement in the
same newspaper, his rates were listed as one pound for a single man
to Baltimore or 7s/6d for a single man to Annapolis. Mileage factored
into the fee schedule.

On his way to the same Congress, George Washington left Alexandria by ferry on May 4, 1775 and lodged at Marlborough, Maryland.
From there he ferried across the Patapsco at Baltimore and then to
Havre de Grace, where he took the Lower Ferry across the Susquehanna.

The eighteenth-century ferries crossing the bay had sails, and passage could be hindered by the weather. When Tench Tilghman, Washington's aide-de-camp, crossed on the ferry in 1781, calm waters de-

The Whitehaven Ferry still takes passengers across the Wicomico River.

layed his trip to Philadelphia with the news that "Cornwallis is taken." In September 1790, Secretary of State Thomas Jefferson and Congressman James Madison waited all day on the shore of Gray's Inn Creek to board a ferry for Annapolis. They spent their time talking, strolling, rowing, and feasting on crabs.

These ferries across the bay were hubs of activity during the Revolutionary War. The government hired them to transport food (pork, bacon, fish, flour), clothing (especially shoes), and muskets. In December 1778, James Claypoole of Chestertown wrote to the Maryland Council of Safety that two hundred pairs of shoes had been sent on the Rock Hall boat and that he could send two hundred more in four weeks.[8] In addition to transporting needed goods, ferrymen were expected to apprehend all deserters or escaped military prisoners trying to cross; those who failed to do so faced fines. The military impressed ferryboats and their owners to transport troops and horses, and ferrymen received chits, or certificates, that promised payment at some later date. The emerging nation had little money to run a war, yet

CHESAPEAKE FERRIES

as time went on some ferrymen refused to transport on credit until they received hard cash. One quartermaster pleaded with Maryland's governor for regulations that guaranteed payment for the ferrymen. Without such laws, the army depended upon the "unreasonable Humour of the Keepers of many of the ferrys."[9]

Two of the ferries in use at the time of the American Revolution are still in operation today, the Whitehaven Ferry and Upper Ferry crossing the Wicomico River. The Whitehaven Ferry crosses the Wicomico River about ten miles from where the river enters the bay and is listed on the Department of Interior's National Register of Historic Places. The town of Whitehaven, founded in 1688, quickly developed as an important tobacco port. Tobacco growers shipped from Whitehaven before that date, as noted in Thomas Willin's will. His estate included three thousand pounds of tobacco being kept at the county ferry, a clear indication that the ferry existed prior to 1688 when Whitehaven officially gained status as a town. With its thirty-four-foot-deep port, the town grew and prospered, and by the late nineteenth century was a shipbuilding and transportation center. The town produced barges and pontoons during World War I and burgeoned with the influx of journeymen. The most recent burst of activity can be traced to the 1920s, when there was an active rum-running trade for about three years.

The Whitehaven Ferry House, a two-story, gambrel-roofed building, sits at the river's edge by the ferry ramp. It was built by Wicomico County for the convenience and comfort of the ferryman, though this is a busy enterprise with constant traffic and the ferryman scarcely gets a chance to pause. The early wooden cable boats were powered across the Wicomico River by a notched heaver and later by a small tug. The first steel boat had a jet drive, then was powered by outboard motors. A steel cable boat powered by a diesel engine now serves as the free ferry. It holds three cars and six people, the maximum permitted by the Coast Guard for an uninspected vessel. There are signs at the water's edge on the Whitehaven side warning other boaters about the cable crossing the river.

As its name implies, the Upper Ferry is up the river from the Whitehaven, about six miles from Salisbury. In the eighteenth century it served as a main link on the stage road from Princess Anne to Vienna and points north. Originally established and operated as a toll ferry by the Handy family, it is presently operated by Wicomico County free to all users, and is propelled by an outboard motor and guided by a cable. Both the Upper Ferry and Whitehaven operate daily, weather permitting. The same phenomena that beset all ferries—lightning, exceptionally high or low tides, fog, and ice—give these scows pause.

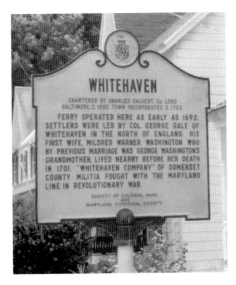

This sign provides a reminder of the Whitehaven ferry's long history.

This pamphlet cover depicts a twentieth-century ferry crossing the Chesapeake Bay.

The county has established a phone message regarding inclement-weather closing to aid commuters. Of course, the modern traveler can just turn the car around and find a bridge route if the ferry is not running, but not so his predecessors who waited for fair weather, whiling away the time at the races, rowing around the harbor, tippling at the ordinary, or as best they could.

CHAPTER 7

Upper Bay Ferries

"Well calculated for the Accomodation of Paffengers"

Some of the most historic ferries on the Upper Bay crossed the Y-shaped Susquehanna River. The river's drainage basin covers 27,500 miles, over half of it in Pennsylvania. From its origin at Lake Otsego, New York, the Susquehanna runs a distance of 448 miles to Havre de Grace, Maryland, where it enters the Chesapeake Bay and supplies 50 percent of the freshwater to the estuary. This river, among the longest non-navigable rivers in the world, contains shallow lower reaches filled with rocks that make navigating these spots impossible. During spring freshets, however, these spots are passable. Ferries crossed the river in many places. One source listed seventeen ferries operating in the eighteenth century between Harris' Ferry (Harrisburg, Pennsylvania) and Lower Ferry (Perryville, Maryland), a distance of about sixty-five miles. [1]

One well-traveled route during colonial times was the Great Wagon Road. It extended from Philadelphia to Downingtown, thence to Lancaster, Columbia, York, and Gettysburg, then south to Hagerstown. From there the road crossed the Potomac at Watkin's Ferry and wound south to Virginia. The ferry crossing of the Susquehanna was at present-day Columbia. Quaker John Wright received a charter to operate this ferry in 1730. Wright was a well-off, politically active

Philadelphian who acquired a thousand acres of land on the east side of the river, became a justice of the peace, and named the newly created county after Lancaster, England, from whence he came. He brought his daughter, Susanna, who made Wright's Ferry a unique stopover for the traveler. Susanna had been educated in England in science and medicine, spoke several languages, had a large library, and wrote poetry and essays. Her scientific curiosity led her to successfully raise silkworms. She maintained a lively correspondence with Benjamin Franklin, a long-standing friend. She sent him apples and "Susquehanna Salmon" (pickled pike); he in turn sent her books, candles, and his "regards to all my Friends at the River."[2]

John Wright Jr. maintained the ferry and a tavern on the western shore. Wright's ferry prospered with the high numbers of settlers moving west, and wagon teams often waited two or three days for the ferry. They spent the time buying goods, causing the merchants to re-stock and, as one traveler said, doing "all they can to make hay while the sun shines, or rather to make money while the river is high."[3]

These routes would also prove useful to members of the Continental Congress, then meeting in Philadelphia. In 1777, anticipating the arrival of British troops, the representatives fled west out of Philadelphia, moving from city to city, and finally arriving in York. During that time of travel and resettlement, they worked to raise and administer a Continental army, and wrote several preliminary drafts of the Articles of Confederation. The final version was approved in November 1777.

A few miles north of Wright's Ferry the river makes a bend and becomes narrower and deeper. Just beyond this point, at the site of present-day Marietta, Anderson's Ferry was established. Its shorter crossing made the journey to York quicker, particularly for travelers coming through Reading from the north. There was great rivalry between the two ferries. The Wrights advertised in the *Pennsylvania Chronicle* that their operation was the only good one and they offered a cut-rate price to bolster trade. Jacob Strickler, who owned Anderson's Ferry in 1787, countered that Mr. Wright "knows nothing of a ferry, nor what constitutes it, and is in no wise calculated to be a ferryman." Strickler maintained that Wright waylaid people on the road and persuaded them to use his ferry. He also stated that the boats of the noted Anderson's Ferry were good and new and equal, if not superior, to any on the river.[4]

In 1788 Samuel Wright, a nephew of the original John Wright, re-named Wright's Ferry "Columbia" and laid out one hundred acres in building lots to be sold by lottery. He reserved the riverbank for the ferry and shipping business, and another plot for the United States Capitol building. There was a lot of support to have Columbia so named, and debate became heated. Congressman Thomas Hartley of

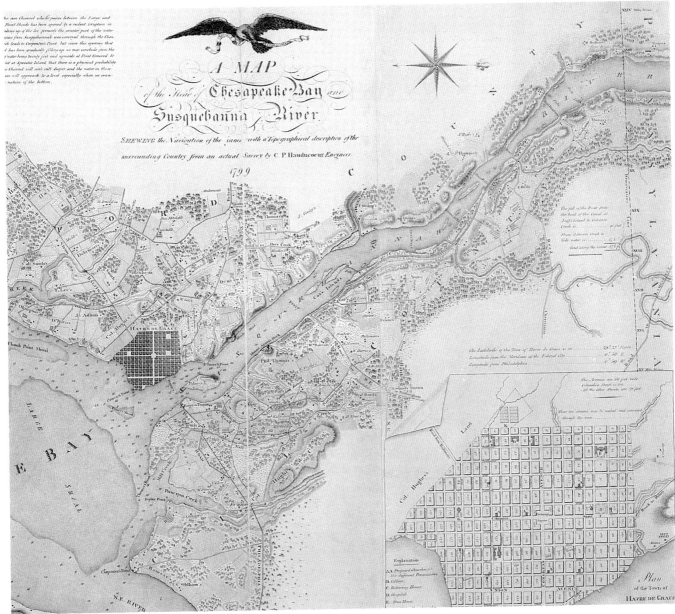

This detail from a 1799 map shows the Susquehanna River flowing south to the Chesapeake Bay.

York spoke of the "prime good fish" that would grace a member's table if the nation's capital were at this commercial center on the Susquehanna.[5] His plea and other arguments failed, of course, and Washington, D.C. was carved out of Maryland.

Columbia, at the end of the navigable Susquehanna, continued to grow and became a major port for coal, timber, grain, and whiskey shipped downriver on shallow, flat-bottomed arks and rafts. Wright's Ferry continued as the crossing until 1812 when the world's longest covered bridge spanned the river. The bridge was destroyed by an ice storm twenty years later, rebuilt, and in 1863 set on fire by local militia to keep the Confederate Army from using it.[6]

A ferry scene on the Susquehanna at Wright's Ferry near Havre de Grace. Watercolor by Pavel Petrovich Svinin, courtesy of the Metropolitan Museum of Art.

The age of steam ushered in many changes, including the Columbia Steam Ferry and Tow Boat Company, which transported passengers, light freight, horses, and buggies from its base in Wrightsville to Columbia. In the 1890s two brothers, Charlie and George Grant, started the service that continued under three sets of owners until 1924. Two propeller-driven boats, *Mary* and *Henry,* were able to cross the river because the dam built below Columbia for the unsuccessful Susquehanna and Tidewater Canal had deepened the river. A number of towboats were used for the freight and buggies. Later, as the dam deteriorated and the river subsided, the company used the *Helen,* a sixteen-foot, flat-bottomed boat. Commuters, salesmen, and tourists used the ferry, which operated from six o'clock in the morning to eight-thirty at night—as did the Columbia Baking Company, which paid twenty cents a day to have baskets of bread ferried to customers.

The best-known ferry south of Wright's was Lower Ferry, located where the broad mouth of the Susquehanna meets the majestic sweep of the headwaters of the Chesapeake. The ferry, a vital link in the post road from Philadelphia to Baltimore, crossed from what is

CHESAPEAKE FERRIES

now Havre de Grace in Harford County to Perryville in Cecil County. Service began October 7, 1695, when Jacob Young and William York appeared before the Baltimore County Council (Harford County was not yet formed) and proposed that they keep a ferry at the mouth of the Susquehanna and an ordinary on each side of the river. William York would do business on the western side and Jacob Young on the east. The council granted the request and determined that they could charge one shilling, six pence for a horse and man. Persons on foot paid one shilling to cross the river. [7] In 1724 the right to operate the ferry was granted to John Stokes, and in 1737 to Humphrey Wells Stokes, who stated in his application that the place where he proposed to do business was "the old ancient place of ferrying and where the main road directly leads to." The ferry had many subsequent owners, including the Philadelphia, Wilmington and Baltimore Railroad Company, which did not bridge the river until 1866.

There was much proselytizing traffic on the post road and many of the journeyers kept diaries. Thomas Chalkley, a Quaker minister, Thomas Lightfoot, and William Brown used the road in 1721 on their way to meeting at Bush River. They found the people at the tavern fiddling and dancing and admonished them that "as many paces as a man takes in his dance, so many steps he takes to hell." Methodist evangelist George Whitefield wrote in 1739 that after crossing the ferry

Anderson's Mill, on the Susquehanna River, below Wright's Ferry.

*The **Mary** traveled between Wrightsville and Columbia.*

he was received in the home of a gentleman who needed salvation. The man had been about to cheer his friends with a "bottle and the bowl" until Whitefield had him substitute family prayer. The self-flagellating missionary Francis Asbury, bishop of the newly organized Methodist Episcopal Church in America, often crossed on the ferry from 1773 to 1815. He once noted that when he came to the ferry he had an agreeable time, calling "on the Lord by prayer in our room at the ferry."[8]

Another diarist, Dr. Alexander Hamilton of Annapolis, visited the area in 1744. He had come to collect some of the ginseng that he heard had been discovered along the river. Hamilton noted that a little old man, who invited him to the family dinner, kept the ferry. Although he did accept a bit of cider, the doctor declined the dinner at the sight of fish with no sauce, no tablecloth, dirty deep wooden dishes, and no spoons.[9] Hopefully the service improved in 1745 when a two-and-one-half-story tavern was built of massive stone at the eastern ferry terminus. In about 1780, Scottish immigrant John Rodgers purchased the ferry and it prospered. He operated a tavern on the western side of the Susquehanna and owned acreage there, including a sawmill and a gristmill. Rodgers Tavern, as it is now known, became a favorite stopover on the post road. When John Rodgers died in 1791 his wife retained the business, which continued under various owners until 1886.[10]

This northeastern area of Maryland was a busy place in the later part of the eighteenth century. Principio Furnace on nearby Principio Creek, an important iron manufacturer since 1715, supplied cannonballs to the Continental army. Elkton, then known as Head of Elk, served as a major army depot. Lieutenant General Sir William Howe knew this and sailed up the Chesapeake Bay in August 1777, laying waste to the countryside from the Sassafras River to the Elk River on his way to capture Philadelphia. George Washington, who was in Wilmington, Delaware, with 11,000 troops hoping to foil Howe's attempt, made a reconnoitering trip to Head of Elk. The British recognized the importance of the area, particularly that of its ferries. In May 1778, Susquehanna River ferries from Harris' to Lower Ferry were surveyed by order of the British War Board. The report prepared from the survey aided in planning troop movement south. Seventeen ferries were listed in the survey. Until 1781 the area saw troops and supplies moved according to the shifting vicissitudes of war, but in that year the upper Chesapeake and its ferries gained prominence in the Continental cause.

In February 1781, Commander-in-Chief George Washington ordered his French ally the Marquis de Lafayette to proceed to Virginia and capture traitorous General Benedict Arnold. Lafayette sailed his infantry and artillery from the Head of Elk to Annapolis only to discover a British blockade that immobilized his troops. The Frenchman proceeded to Virginia to look over the lay of the land. Returning to Annapolis, Lafayette decided that as the British were in command of the Chesapeake Bay, he would evade the blockade and sail his troops back to Head of Elk. There he found orders from Washington to proceed south again. This did not sit at all well with many of the soldiers. They had not been paid for many months, had no shoes, little clothing, and a sparse diet. Most of the Rhode Island regulars deserted and left for home. Lafayette feared others would follow suit, as this time he was going to march, not sail, south. Every stop they made to be ferried across a river would give soldiers a chance to slip away and he worried that half of them would do so. The countryside had been previously scoured for barrels of biscuits, cattle, bacon, vessels with crew, and wood. Now couriers galloped back and forth with letters from the Maryland Council of Safety, Governor Lee, and Lafayette. This time he needed wagons and teams to transport six field pieces, fourteen cannon with tons of shot, shells, and powder, plus whatever foodstuffs could be gleaned from the already ravaged area. Lafayette would march his 1500 troops west, across the Susquehanna River at Bald Friar Ferry and then south to Virginia. It was an uphill, downhill struggle, over undulating terrain, first north from Head of Elk and then west to Bald Friar Ferry located just over a mile south of

The story of the Bald Friar Ferry is memorialized in this sign. Author photo.

the Pennsylvania border. Lafayette chose this spot, now covered by the Conowingo Dam, instead of Lower Ferry, because the river was shallow enough to be forded and they could haul across the artillery.

Lafayette left Head of Elk on April 11, 1781, and marched about twelve miles northwest to Brick Meeting House, where his troops camped for the night. The next day they marched about another twelve miles to Bald Friar. Although fordable, it was, according to one French officer, "diabolique," full of slippery rocks and potholes. Lafayette opted to cross over by scow, but it ran aground. A local man, Aquilla Deaver, rescued him and carried the marquis across the river. When Lafayette made his triumphal return tour to America years later, he and Deaver reminisced. [11]

Once across Bald Friar, Lafayette consulted with his officers about the soldiers' discontent. The officers were aware of strong rumblings from the troops over their lack of shoes and comforts. Lafayette again feared they would desert. He decided to give his troops an example of the cost of a traitorous act and hanged Walter Pigot, a loyalist spy who, posing as a miller, had shipped with the troops from Annapolis and been caught. After the trial, Lafayette wrote to Governor Thomas Sim Lee, "Pigot being convinced of coming within the description of a Spy, was Hanged at Susquehanna Ferry."[12] This must have been a novel experience for the people at the ferry. On April 19, Lafayette ferried across the Patapsco River at Elkridge Landing. One of the scows used for the crossing was so jammed with soldiers that it sank and nine of them drowned. They were on their way to Yorktown and requisitioned boats at Baltimore to sail down the Chesapeake and thus, for a time, avoided ferrying and marching.

Lower Ferry played its part in the winning of the Revolution in September 1781 when Washington and Marshall Rochambeau marched south to hem in Cornwallis at Yorktown. Washington planned to sail south from Head of Elk, but he found a great "deficiency of transports" and sent letters to influential gentlemen on the Eastern Shore asking for vessels and that they gather at Baltimore harbor. He and Rochambeau traveled overland, crossing the teams and horses at Bald Friar Ferry and the troops at Lower Ferry on September 8. They must have crossed in good order for Washington reached Baltimore the following day. On the return trip, however, in August 1782, Calude Blanchard said it took the army two days to cross because there was only one boat at Lower Ferry. Eight years later M. Brissot de Marville wrote of an American trip, noting that there was a good ferryman at Havre de Grace. Over the years the majority of them must have been "good ferrymen" who did their best to oblige passengers in all sorts of weather, despite the conditions of the time.

Isaac Weld Jr., the Irish sojourner, traveled from Mount Vernon to Philadelphia in February 1798, via Lower Ferry, where he and his fellow travelers found the river covered with ice. The ferryman opined that the ice was too thick near the shore to cut and too thin mid-river to cross. No one wanted to spend the night at the west-side ferry house, and so the passengers prevailed upon the ferryman to give ice-breaking a try. Twelve passengers, four horses, and the seven-man crew got in the boat. The crew stood in the bow of the boat beating the ice with clubs, whilst the others using iron-headed poles endeavored to push the boat forward. After two hours of this shivering struggle they found themselves in a boat frozen mid-river. Weld saved the day by firing his pistols to alert people on the shore who sent a small flat-bottomed bateau to their aid. The bateau was put in front of the ferryboat and they rocked it back and forth. This action broke the ice bit by bit and the larger boat could follow. After three and a half hours of such travel, Weld and company reached shore and the tavern's welcome hearth.[13]

Packet boats came into use on the upper Chesapeake Bay by the end of the eighteenth century. In a May 1793 issue of the Chestertown *Apollo*, John Constable and James Piper advertised that on their packet:

> The Cabin is large and commodious, well calculated for the Accomodation of Paffengers, Merchandife, Produce, &c. caried on the loweft Terms . . . Will regularly leave Chefertown every MONDAY at Nine o'clock, A.M. and fet out for Baltimore, every THURSDAY, at Nine o'clock, A.M.

The Baltimore steamship F. C. Latrobe.

The invention of steam-powered boats also changed the travel mode in the upper reaches of the Chesapeake Bay. It did not take men long to devise ways to cash in on this new invention. The one-hundred-thirty-seven-foot side-wheeler *Chesapeake*, equipped with one smokestack and one mast and sail, was built in Baltimore in 1813 and began a regular Monday—Wednesday—Friday run across the bay to Frenchtown, Maryland, on the Elk River. The passengers transferred to a stagecoach that took them to New Castle, Delaware, from whence they boarded another steamboat for a ride up the Delaware River to Philadelphia. The side-wheelers soon took away the business of the sailing packets. Mederic-Louis-Elie Moreau de Saint-Mery's description of his trip in 1794 gives an excellent picture of the tidewater travel of his time. He left Baltimore at 8:30 A.M. on a sailing schooner that held twenty-five passengers. The six berths he had reserved for his party were to be marked with chalk, but he found only four of them so designated, the other two usurped. After much exhortation with the captain, Moreau de Saint-Mery got the cabins back—fortunately, as they did not arrive in Frenchtown on the Elk until 1:00 A.M. There they waited until about five o'clock when a scow came to take them and their luggage to land where they boarded stages for the ride to New Castle, Delaware. Eight miles later they stopped in Glasgow to water the horses and thirteen miles later came another stop, again to water the horses. Six miles later they reached New Castle where they boarded another vessel to sail up the Delaware River to Philadelphia. In spite of stops and delays, people hailed the shortened travel time and the steamboat.[14]

By the later part of the nineteenth century, tidewater Virginia and tidewater Maryland were infested with steamboats plying the great rivers and bay, stopping at town wharves along the way to take on passengers and freight. There were overnight passages on vessels fitted with staterooms for travelers going a distance and also excursions to resorts.

Commuter ferrying developed and expanded. In 1813, one Peter Paul ferried people across Baltimore Harbor. By 1851, the Locust Point Ferry Company used a steam ferry to traverse the harbor, and by 1868 citizens were complaining that steam ferry competition swamped the small boats still actively ferrying shoppers and vehicles in order to shorten the ride on the rough roads around the harbor. When in the first half of the twentieth century, the Baltimore Harbor Board ran auto ferries from Broadway to Locust Point for workers at the Bethlehem-Fairfield Shipyard, people complained about the parked cars in their neighborhood. The cross-harbor service ceased in 1939, its demise due to the arrival of the streetcar which made commuting easier.

"The Harbor, Baltimore" is an etching by Sears Gallagher.

The Baltimore and Ohio Railroad started the Canton Car Ferry across Baltimore Harbor when the Pennsylvania Railroad no longer accepted passage of B & O trains on their direct line from Baltimore to Philadelphia. The railroad established a car ferry across the harbor from its Locust Point terminal to a slip at Third Avenue west of Clinton Street. The railroad used two large ferries, the *John W. Garrett* and the *Canton*. This method of transferring passenger and freight cars operated until 1895 when the B & O Railroad's use of the Howard Street tunnel created an all-rail route through the city.

CHAPTER 8

Railroad and Automobile Ferries

"Facilities available to handle anything permitted over the highways"

The development and expansion of the railroad system would have far-reaching effects on transportation and other areas of American life. The first railroad was organized in 1827, and in 1829 the first locomotive built in America, the Tom Thumb, had its trial run. In 1830, the first passenger and freight station was established, at Mount Clare, in Baltimore. Rail travel would progress from horse-drawn carriages, rolling along rails, to steam power, which soon replaced horse power.

The system expanded quickly. Iron rails were being laid for track and small railroad companies carrying passengers short distances sprang up all over the map. One of these, the Frenchtown and New Castle Railroad Company, used horse power for the first two years of its existence and then switched to steam in 1833. This line ran the same route from Frenchtown to New Castle that the stages had used, but in far less time. By 1838, the Philadelphia, Wilmington, and New Castle Railroad, an amalgamation of several small railroads, took over the Frenchtown and New Castle. This acquisition ushered in a unique travel system that combined the thriving ferries and railroads on the upper and lower reaches of the Chesapeake Bay. Just as eighteenth-century travelers crossed the Susquehanna on Lower Ferry, the Philadelphia,

The Salisbury train disturbs a cypress swamp.

Wilmington, and Baltimore Railroad passengers crossed the river on the car ferry *Susquehanna*. Built in Baltimore in 1837, the side-wheeler included a single railroad track on its upper deck and room for passengers on the main deck. Upon reaching the river, the train stopped and the passengers disembarked and walked to board the *Susquehanna*. While on board, passengers could partake of refreshments in the main salon while ferrymen loaded the railroad cars. Engines, due to their weight, did not travel on car ferry. The crossing, including passenger exchanges, was listed on the company's timetable as taking one and one-quarter hours.

In 1838, actress Fanny Kemble wrote of a winter trip from Philadelphia to Baltimore on which the steamboat cut through the one-inch-thick ice on the Susquehanna River with ease. In 1850, Matilda C. Houstoun described a trip on the same route as uninteresting and tiresome. She noted that the sun blazed into the many train windows.

CHESAPEAKE FERRIES

The windows had no blinds, there was no fresh air, and a red-hot stove sat in the middle of the car. She added that upon reaching the river "We all left the land conveyance . . . and were hustled on board a sort of covered raft, which was then propelled by steam across the Susquehanna River." She stated that people fought for the minimal sitting room.[1]

The most amazing railroad-to-ferry-to-railroad trips were in the winter of 1852, when between January 15 and February 24 the ice was so thick on the Susquehanna River that no car ferry could cross. The Philadelphia, Wilmington, and Baltimore Railroad put tracks across the ice and pulled the cars with cables—1,378 cars from one side of the frozen river to the other. In this same year, the *Susquehanna* ran 1,372 miles, a high number of ferry miles. The railroad company applied for permission to bridge the river and ordered a new ferry, the *Maryland*, described as "the new iron ferryboat." She was a true car ferry, 220 feet long with a 35-foot beam. The boat had two tracks on the top deck, could transport an entire passenger train in one trip, and spanned the river in eight minutes. The company provided a new covered walkway to the vessel for the passengers who rode in the salon. The *Maryland* continued ferrying during the Civil War and in April 1861 conveyed Benjamin F. Butler and his Eighth Massachusetts Infantry down the bay to Annapolis from whence they planned to march to Washington, D.C.[2] After starts and delays, the Philadelphia, Wilmington, and Baltimore Railroad opened their bridge across the Susquehanna River on November 22, 1866, and retired the *Maryland* from ferry service.[3] For almost thirty years the railroad transferred cars to a ferry and then back to land again, all for the lack of a trestle bridge.

A similar railroad-to-ferry-to-railroad system developed at the southern end of the Chesapeake Bay in 1884 when the New York,

This detail of a poster for the Adams Express Company shows the railroad tracks across the frozen Susquehanna that were necessary in the winter of 1852.

Philadelphia, and Norfolk Railroad began ferrying railroad cars, passengers, and freight from the Eastern Shore of Virginia to Norfolk. The New York, Philadelphia, and Norfolk Railroad Company, later known affectionately as the "NiP 'n N," was the fulfillment of the dream of two Pennsylvanians, William L. Scott and Alexander J. Cassatt.[4] These men envisioned building a railroad that would connect with existing lines on Maryland's Eastern Shore and run down to the tip of Virginia's peninsula, where passengers would be conveyed to a boat and ferried across the bay. This grand scheme would make it possible for travelers to go from New York to Florida comfortably and speedily.

Unable to interest the Pennsylvania Railroad in their venture, Cassatt and Scott invested their own money, bought up smaller companies, and plotted their route. In 1881, Cassatt, an engineer (and later president of the Pennsylvania Railroad), surveyed the peninsula, beset by townspeople who wanted the road routed through their hamlets. Cassatt ignored them all and drew a straight line down the middle of the peninsula, bypassing all of the seaside and bayside spots. Scott purchased 2,000 acres south of Cherrystone Wharf and laid out the new town of Cape Charles City, the future terminus of the railroad and the landing place for the ferries. The ferry steamer docked at the wharf, on which there was an open pavilion. Passengers simply stepped off the train that ran parallel to the wharf, walked across, and boarded the ferry. Service began on November 17, 1884, with the side-wheeler *Jane Mosely* carrying freight and passengers across the bay. The company's owners also planned to ferry railroad cars, and in 1885 the tug *Norfolk* towed a wooden car float carrying twelve freight cars across the bay. Cassatt designed a steel-hull barge to carry freight cars, and ferrying car floats became an important part of the company's business. When the Pennsylvania Railroad took over the road, the company's inventory listed eighteen barges, three steamships, and ten tugs. In 1885 the company added the modern steamboat *Cape Charles*, a ship that could do about eighteen knots, had two railroad tracks, a Pullman car, and a shorter car. The intention was to spare passengers the bother of transferring to the ferry. This did not prove popular with passengers, however, who preferred getting off the railroad, onto a boat, and then back onto the railroad as they had done at Lower Susquehanna Ferry before the Civil War. The "stay in the comfort of your Pullman car" run lasted just one year.

The company operated ferryboats with green hulls and railings and red superstructures until 1900 when they added the *Pennsylvania* and painted all of the vessels white. In September 1884 an advertisement in Maryland's *Salisbury Advertiser* stated "We have been looking over the time card of the New York, Philadelphia, and Norfolk Rail Road to

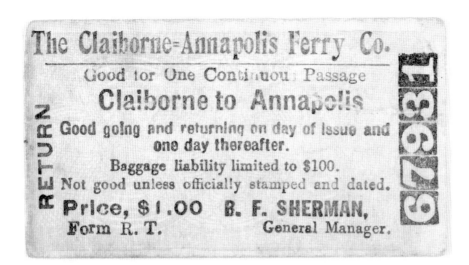

find out the method of its schedule. It seems to be arranged for the purpose of making it hard to get anywhere or after getting there to get back."[5] The "NiP 'n N" prospered, however, ferrying higher numbers of passengers and towing more barges loaded with freight cars. In 1928, *Virginia Lee* was added to the line, labeled the finest steamboat that ever plied the bay and as handsome as an ocean liner. The boat stretched 300 feet in length and held 80 cars. The elegant dining room boasted fine linen, sparkling glassware, fancy china, and uniformed waiters serving delicious food. Passengers relaxed in comfort on any of the three daily trips.

The most serious threats to ferry navigation on the lower bay were bad weather and traffic on the two main channels. As at many ferry crossings, fog and ice presented the worst problems. In 1893 the thick ice trapped the steamer *New York* and the tug *Norfolk*. They remained thus for twenty-four hours, going with the floe until the mate of the *New York* walked to shore, telegraphed for help, and had two tugs come to the rescue—a far different solution from the one Isaac Weld had written of a hundred years earlier when all hands worked to free an iced-in sailing ferry.

The bay crossing took almost three hours in good weather. Travelers crossed making rail connections and those on excursion from Norfolk to Cape Charles dallied three hours and then returned home. Later, of course, automobiles used the ferry. It was a prosperous endeavor, and in 1934 the Pennsylvania Railroad incorporated the New York, Philadelphia, and Norfolk Railroad Ferry Company. In 1944 its two boats, *Elisha Lee* and *Maryland* carried more than one million passengers across the bay. At Christmastime that year, three thousand travelers crowded the wharf at one time, but after the end of World War II the route was used less and less, profits plummeted, and

The steamer Talbot, *at the wharf in Cambridge, Maryland, graces an old postcard.*

on February 28, 1953, *Elisha Lee* made the route's last trip from Cape Charles to Old Point Comfort and Norfolk.

On April 1, 1933, the Virginia Ferry Corporation, a subsidiary of the Pennsylvania Railroad, began passenger-automobile ferry service from Little Creek on Norfolk's bayside to Cape Charles. Local newspapers hailed the event with headlines such as "Better Ferry Service Begins," and carried advertisements emphasizing three round-trips daily for passenger cars and light trucks, and two round-trips for heavy trucks and equipment towed on barges.[6] The Virginia Ferry Corporation replaced the Peninsula Ferry Corporation running between Pine Beach and Cape Charles. The new run began with the railroad's old steamer *Pennsylvania*, but the company replaced the older boat as soon as possible with the 250-foot steamboat *Del-Mar-Va*. The new boat, designed for the route, had bow and stern loading, six lanes for cars, and "facilities available to handle anything permitted over the highways." The ferry did not have to turn around when docking cars and could therefore unload quickly. Motorists liked this time-saving feature and adopted this new route that connected two segments of U.S. Route 13. Route 13 ran from Maine to Florida, from "Pine to Palm," and travelers used it to avoid the crawling drive through some cities, onerous in the pre-beltway, pre-air-conditioning driving days. [7] More ships and longer schedules followed until five ferries ran the twenty-one-mile crossing, each in one hour and twenty-five minutes.

In 1950, the Virginia Fe
terminus from Cape Charl
peninsula. To create a harl
World War II concrete shi
headed pier with loading
the Virginia Ferry Corpora
restaurant. This new harbc
miles. Automobile traffic s
senger and mail trains dc
railroad office at Cape Ch.
was razed. Kiptopeke Stat
ries docked from 1950 to
Tunnel.

The company lengthen
of automobiles. The vene
ey, was increased by seve
wealth of Virginia had ta
Chesapeake Bay Ferry C
had seven vessels runnii
doomed the service. The
sion was formed in Septe
new bridge. On April 14
nel opened. The comple
man-made eight-acre is
nels, and two bridges. I
that the state funded a
opened in the spring of
in 2000.

That same April 14 must have been a sad day for an ferry enthu-siasts. At 8:05 P.M., the *Pocahontas* steamed out of Kiptopeke on its last trip. The ferry stretched 376 feet in length, held 120 cars, 1,200 passengers, and a crew of 39 and reached Little Creek at 9:35 P.M. The ferry service that had thrived since the early days of sail-powered skiffs thus ended. The Delaware River and Bay Authority renamed the ferry *Delaware* and ran it from Lewes, Delaware, to Cape May, New Jersey. It should be noted that, fittingly, the route used by the bridge-tunnel parallels that used by the ferries.

Enterprising entrepreneurs also combined ferry and railroad travel in the upper part of the bay. The steamer *Tockwogh* of the Baltimore and Eastern Railroad ran from Bay Ridge near Annapolis to Claiborne

The Love Point Hotel on Kent Island.

in Talbot County, Maryland. The railroad began in 1890 with a line completed from Claiborne to Ocean City on the Atlantic Ocean. The railroad obtained the ferry *Thames River* to carry eight loaded freight cars across the bay and ran its first trip on November 11, 1890. They added the *Olive* to carry passengers. On October 5, 1891, the company switched the western terminus from Annapolis to Baltimore, and used the *B. S. Ford* for this run. The railroad suffered financial difficulties from its beginning and went out of business in 1894.

In 1894, the Queen Anne's Railroad Company was incorporated in Centreville, Maryland, and ran a line through Queen Anne's, Talbot, and Caroline Counties to Lewes, Delaware. From there, passengers traveled by steamer to Cape May, New Jersey. The side-wheeler ferry *Queen Anne*, launched with much hoopla and a release of white doves in 1899, operated from Pier 9½ on Light Street in Baltimore. The ferry carried passengers across the bay, stopping at Kent Island and docking at Queenstown on the Chester River in Queen Anne's County, where riders boarded the train that took them to the end of the line in 2½ hours. If passengers did not disembark at stations along the way, they had five hours to enjoy the Delaware Bay at Lewes before catching the return trip to Baltimore. In 1902, the Chesapeake Bay terminus was changed from Queenstown to Love Point on Kent Island. By 1902 the company had added additional vessels to the line and the schedule listed three round-trips a day. The trip was a popular outing in the warmer months for families who boarded the ferries out of Baltimore dressed in their finery and toted baskets of food, ready to make a long day's outing. Nevertheless, the Queen Anne's Railroad was not profit-

Two views of the steamship Emma Giles, *which delivered countless vacationers to Love Point.*

The steamship Cambridge.

able and in 1905 became part of the Maryland, Delaware, and Virginia Railway Company. The "Many Dirty Visits," as the railroad was known, continued the Chesapeake Bay ferry service, but eliminated the steamer to Cape May, New Jersey. Always vulnerable in inclement weather, one of the ferries, *Westmoreland,* steamed past the Love Point landing on a foggy day. An alert railroad man climbed a locomotive and pulled the whistle until the boat's lights showed she was turning around and coming into port.[8] This steamer-to-railroad line, a close duplicate of the Baltimore, Chesapeake, Atlantic Railway, was sold in 1923.

The Baltimore, Chesapeake, and Atlantic Railway (or "Black, Cinders, and Ashes"), yet another steamer-and-railroad combination company, served excursionists during the summer months and maintained a good passenger and freight business during the off season. Service began in 1894 and the steamship *Cambridge* ferried passengers across the bay from Baltimore's Light Street to Claiborne in Talbot County. There the ferry met the crack express, *Baltimore Flyer,* that sped to Ocean City, Maryland, in just over two hours. *Cambridge* continued the run three times a day for thirty years. In 1924, the Eastern Shore terminus was moved from Claiborne to Love Point and featured *Cambridge* on the new run. As a popular resort, Love Point attracted visitors to the Love Point and Philmore Hotels, the Dream Land Amusement Park, and a casino. On summer Sundays as many as three steamers docked at the wharf, and the hotel served fish, chicken, and crab dinners to 540 hungry diners in just two hours and forty minutes. The relative comfort and ease of steamer-railroad travel appealed to more and more travel-minded people. Shorter work weeks and the increase in automobile use added to this wanderlust.

In the early twentieth century there was still only one way to get across the bay—by ferry—and the companies that catered to excursionists shifted their attention to automobile travelers. More and more people owned cars or traveled by bus and wanted to be able to get up and go, even across the waters. In 1931, the Baltimore and Eastern Railroad which had been running *Cambridge* from Baltimore to Love Point added the car ferry *Philadelphia* to the line. Advertisements for the screw, double-ended vessel emphasized "Drive-On, Drive-Off." A 1934 brochure listed the times of three daily round-trips from Pier 5, Light Street, Baltimore, with one-way passenger rates at sixty-five

The steamship **Cambridge** *approaches the dock at Claiborne.*

cents. The boat hauled autos and trucks on all trips. Other rates included car, $2.50; bus, $5.00; trucks, $4.00–$7.00 (based on size); motorcycle, $1.00, $1.50 with sidecar. This timetable also noted that "steamers (operated) between Baltimore and Love Point weather and tide permitting," and included the caveat that the company was not responsible for any damage or inconvenience resulting from delay.[9] Although there were other steamers added to the line, *Philadelphia* became a favorite. Families used it again and again and enjoyed picnics and crab feasts on board as the steamer chugged across the bay belching the black smoke that earned it the sobriquet *Smokey Joe*. The boat made its last trip from Love Point at 8:00 P.M. on August 31, 1947.

Over the decades, ferry routes shifted or were discontinued. An exception is the Oxford-Bellevue Ferry across the Tred Avon River. Authorized in 1683, it remains active. Ferry service in the area began when the county court granted Richard Royston ferry rights. For a levy of twenty-five hundred pounds of tobacco a year, Royston served

The **Cambridge II** *at Claiborne, with a train on the other side of the dock.*

ships riding at anchor as well as passengers "on board any Shippe Nigh there Riding."[10] Ferry service continued under other operators, but ceased for a brief period in the 1690s when the county cut off its funding and told one Isaac Sassarson to charge whatever the traffic would bear. Public outcry that citizens were "discommoded by the discontinuance of the Ferry"[11] caused the county to resume its subsidy. In 1721 the court admonished the ferryman to keep a boat sufficient for men and horses, to set over three times a day on a regular schedule or when anyone came to his house, and to carry all who came on Sunday on their way to church. The ferryman was not to run around town seeking passengers, but to sound his horn to announce that the boat was available. The Bennett family operated the wooden, oar-propelled scow for forty years, from 1700–1740. Judith Bennett was married to three different ferrymen and operated the service herself between marriages. Catherine Bennett took over in 1737 and was the first person to be paid in cash instead of with a tobacco subsidy.

In the first half of the eighteenth century, Oxford thrived as a port of entry, but its importance declined after the Revolution. Regular ferry crossings ceased for over fifty years. In the 1830s the town prospered once again and regular ferry service resumed. In 1886 a small steam-driven tug, *William H. Fisher*, towing a wooden scow, was installed as the ferry. A signal system was established on each shore consisting of squares painted black or white. If a passenger was on foot, the signalman raised the black side and the ferryman came in the steamer. But if there was a horse or wagon to cross, he hoisted the white board and the tug towed the scow. The boat developed leaks over the years and had to be pumped out every morning, yet the system worked into the early years of the twentieth century. Finally, in about 1912, the gasoline-driven tug *Vivian* replaced the *William H. Fisher*. The tug plied back and forth until 1931. The county could not afford repairs

in the Depression-era economy and ceased service. Oxford waterman Captain Buck Richardson came to the county's aid and agreed to build a new boat and keep the ferry running if the county would grant him fifteen hundred dollars a year. Thus came into being the fifty-foot, gasoline-powered *Tred Avon* built in Captain Al Sparklin's Oxford boatyard. Richardson's sons ran the ferry for six years until February 21, 1938, when Captain William L. Benson took it over and ran it for the next thirty-six years. In December 1973, Captain Benson announced his retirement and advertised the ferryboat and business for sale. He received nineteen offers and sold it to Captain Gilbert Clark, whose family had kept a ferry between Shelter Island and Long Island, New York for five generations. By 2005 the ferry was still privately owned and operated daily for most of the year. Inclement weather, that bane of all ferrymen, keeps it closed during the winter months.

Early in the twentieth century, while the Oxford-Bellevue continued its Tred Avon crossing, farsighted politicians recognized the growing importance of motor travel. In 1916, the Maryland General Assembly authorized $50,000 to the State Roads Commission for a ferry service across the bay from Annapolis to Claiborne.[12] World War I interrupted the process, but in 1919 Governor Emerson C. Harrington and Attorney General Albert C. Ritchie agreed that an interested group of New York investors could use the funds to start up the ferry system. By the terms of the agreement, the roads commission approved the boat, the state owned and controlled the terminals, and the company provided three round-trips a day during the summer months and two round-trips at other times. On June 19, 1919, the 201-foot side-wheeler *Thomas Patten* was rechristened *Governor Emerson C. Harrington* by the governor's wife. At the christening ceremony the governor noted that "the two shores are at last brought closer together." The mayor of Annapolis presented the state flag to the ferry, a buffet luncheon was served, and the enterprise began.[13]

This new venture floundered. Part of the problem was that roads were generally poor. B. Frank Sherman was hired as general manager of the privately held Claiborne-Annapolis Ferry Company. Sherman devoted the rest of his working career to efficiently managing the ferry system. Several state officials owned shares in the company, but it remained private until 1940.

The owners added the *Albert C. Ritchie* in 1926; it could carry seventy-five cars. The *John M. Dennis*, the company's first new boat, was added in 1929 and could carry one hundred. Ultimately, five diesel-powered ferries operated in continuous service. The Red Star Bus Line began using the ferry in 1928 and carried passengers to Stevensville, Denton, Cambridge, and Salisbury, Maryland, and Rehoboth Beach, Delaware. Bus and car traffic increased and prompted talk of cutting a canal through Kent Island. The waterway would trim forty minutes off the trip from Annapolis to Claiborne. Instead, the company moved the eastern terminus in 1930 to Matapeake on Kent Island, just a few miles below Broad Creek from whence the ferries had sailed in colonial times. For the convenience of waiting passengers, Matapeake had a clubhouse with a dining hall.

On July 1, 1930, the opening of this new terminus was celebrated with a military and civic parade from Stevensville to Matapeake. The ambassadors of England, Holland, Belgium, Brazil, the prince and princess of Italy, and local dignitaries from across the state and county

The Governor Harry W. Nice *Ferry pulls into the dock with a load of cars.*

joined a crowd of more than ten thousand people. There were bands, a pageant, a concert, and fourteen floats, including Father Neptune and the Goddess of Wisdom. A fast-moving squall brought pouring rain just as the last float passed the reviewing stand.[14] Spectators and participants fled in all directions and the newspapers remarked that the governor, literally speechless, could not deliver his dedication remarks.

In 1938 the route to Claiborne was suspended and a shuttle ferry took travelers going south from Romancoke on Kent Island across Eastern Bay to Claiborne. In 1943 the western terminus was moved from Annapolis to Sandy Point which made for a shorter, more efficient, and more frequent run. Automobile traffic increased and during the summer months the line of cars waiting for the ferry often stretched more than a mile. The word "bridge" was frequently used in discussions regarding the best way to accommodate the increasingly heavy traffic. As early as 1907, Baltimore businessman Peter J. Campbell first talked of spanning the Chesapeake. H. L. Mencken, *Baltimore Sun* editor, author, and critic, in his satiric wisdom commented that there simply was not enough traffic between the Eastern and Western Shores to warrant a bridge.

Construction of the Chesapeake Bay Bridge from Sandy Point, 1950.

Traffic starts across the Chesapeake Bay Bridge as the last Matapeake Ferry heads to Sandy Point, 1952.

Nevertheless, the state authorized funds for a bridge in 1947. It opened on July 31, 1952 and its two lanes paralleled part of the ferry's route. Governor Theodore R. McKeldin and B. Frank Sherman rode the *Herbert R. O'Conor* on the last trip, at 5:30 p.m. from Matapeake to Sandy Point. The governor then rushed to the bridge to shake the hand of the driver of the first car across. Ironically, a ferry seems to have had the final word. While the bridge was under construction, a broken steering cable forced the *John M. Dennis* off its course and the boat rammed a pier of the new bridge. The headline read "Boat Bites Bridge." In truth, the ferry service had run since its inception without a major accident which is certainly a tribute to the acumen of its bay captains and crews. But the ferry service, subject to the vagaries of weather, had not run without incident. In December 1940, the *Harry W. Nice* became icebound and seventy passengers and fifty autos were stuck in cold isolation until the U.S. Coast Guard rescued them the next morning—a memorable incident in the history of the Matapeake ferry.

The bridge proved to be popular. The spate of motorists rushing to reach the beach clogged the roads and, on holiday weekends, cars backed up for miles to cross the bridge. In time, regular weekend traffic also caused jams and slowdowns. Maryland, like Virginia, built a parallel span that opened in June 1973. The day of the ferryman was over, yet thankfully, a few small ferries still operate in Virginia and Maryland, offering twenty-first-century travelers the pleasure of fair weather ferrying.

Appendix

Following is a list of Chesapeake ferries cited in research material between the years of 1636 and 2000. The list includes the name, body of water crossed, and available identifying information.

This list by no means encompasses all ferries. (Several important ferries, such as the Tolchester Ferry, were not included.) Many sail- and hand-powered ferries existed in the seventeenth and eighteenth centuries for which there is little information. For example, in 1705 the Virginia General Assembly listed twenty ferries over the James River, twenty over the York River, eight over the Rappahannock River, one over the Potomac River, and two on Virginia's Eastern Shore, identifying them from point to point. Listings such as "at usual place on each side of river," "over to the Row," "burford's to old Talbot's," make positive identification a Herculean task. By 1748 the number of ferries had doubled, the listings still as terse. This list, then, is intended to merely give an idea of the scope of ferrying down through the centuries.

Adams Ferry Potomac River. Auto, bus, passenger steam ferry from Potomac Beach, Westmoreland Co., Virginia. to Morgantown, Charles Co., Maryland. Operated by Captain John Quincy Adams, 1927–1940.

Addison's Ferry Potomac River. Connected Addison's Maryland land with that of Hugh West, Alexandria, Fairfax Co., Virginia. First half of 1700s.

Akers' Ferry Choptank River. Cambridge, Dorchester Co., to Talbot Co., Maryland. Dan Akers was paid fifty pounds a year to operate, 1788.

Anderson's Ferry Susquehanna River. Marietta, Lancaster Co., Pennsylvania. William Anderson got permit to run ferry first half of 1700s. Run by Jacob Strickler in 1780s. Also known as Glatz' Ferry. Listed in report prepared for Gen. Charles Cornwallis 1778.

Ayres' Ferry Chesapeake Bay. Rock Hall, Kent County, Maryland to Annapolis and Baltimore. Abram Ayres advertised in the *Maryland Gazette*, 1769.

Bald Friar Ferry Susquehanna River. Crossing in Cecil County, Maryland two miles below the Mason-Dixon Line. Begun 1695. Used by Lafayette and Rochambeau, 1781. Listed in report prepared for Gen. Charles Cornwallis 1778. Now covered by Conowingo Dam.

Baltimore, Chesapeake, and Atlantic Railway Chesapeake Bay. Railway ran passenger ferries connecting route from Baltimore to Claiborne, Talbot County, Maryland, 1894–1923.

Baltimore and Eastern Shore Railroad Chesapeake Bay. Steam ferries connected with railroad from Annapolis with one at Claiborne, Talbot County, Maryland, 1890–1894.

Baltimore–Love Point Ferry Chesapeake Bay. Baltimore to Love Point, Kent Island, Queen Anne's County, Maryland. Operated by the Baltimore and Eastern Railroad Co., 1924–1947.

Beckworth's Ferry Patuxent River. Calvert County, Maryland. Established by order of Charles Calvert. Operated by George Beckworth, from Point Patience to his home and back weather permitting; Beckworth was to keep sufficient men and boats, apprehend runaway servants, and only charge ferriage decreed by the court, 1672–1675. Later operated by ferrymen Richard Keene and Richard Broughton, who solicited the court for a license in 1680. Court ordered that anyone not licensed must forbear to keep a ferry at the same location.

Bell's Ferry Susquehanna River. Robert Bell bought Smith's Ferry, which ran between Port Deposit, Cecil County and Lapidum, Harford County, Maryland 1793–1828.

Benedict Ferry Patuxent River. Run by Captain Peter "Perry" C. Henderson to Holland Point, Maryland in 1930s.

Berry's Ferry Potomac River. Zachariah Berry and his descendants operated or rented the West Ferry from Annapolis, Maryland to Oxon Hill, Maryland in the 1870s.

Best Pitch Ferry Transquaking River. Rope ferry, Dorchester County, Maryland, mentioned by Footner (1944) *Rivers of the Eastern Shore*.

Blackford's Ferry Potomac River. Sharpsburg, Washington County, Maryland to Shepherdstown, West Virginia. Kept by Colonel John Blackford, first half of the nineteenth century.

Blew (Blue) Rock Ferry Susquehanna River. Four miles below Wrightsville, Pennsylvania. Listed in report prepared for Gen. Charles Cornwallis, 1778. Thomas Cresap received patent from Lord Baltimore to establish ferry in 1730.

Bohemia Ferry   Bohemia River. Cecil County, Maryland. Bassett family kept a tavern at the ferry, eighteenth century. Act of 1763 made provision for tobacco to be inspected at Bohemia Ferry.

Bohemia Old Ferry   Bohemia River. Cecil County, Maryland. Located about where Route 213 now crosses the river. Used by Dr. Alexander Hamilton, 1744.

Bowdoin's Ferry   Chesapeake Bay. Northampton County, Virginia to Norfolk, Hampton, Yorktown. Bought from Eyre family, 1770s, operated by Bowdoin family until 1824.

Bowie Ferry   Rappahannock River. Begun by James Bowie in 1776, from Port Royal in Caroline County to Francis Conway's place in King George County, Virginia. A ferry ran in this crossing until the bridge was built in 1934.

Bowler's Ferry   Rappahannock River. From Bowler's Wharf, Essex County, Virginia to Suggets Point, Virginia, 1792–1820s. Used by plantations on both sides of the river.

Boyd's Hole Ferry   Potomac River. 1705–late 1700s, between Boyd's Hole and Widow Martin's landing at Maryland Point. Used several times by George Washington during the Revolution.

Boyde's Ferry   Patuxent River. Prince George's County Court issued a license to John Boyde in November 1726 to operate a ferry at Queen Anne's Town. In March 1727 he received a license to operate an ordinary at the ferry.

Brandson's Ferry   Wicomico River. In 1664 Charles County, Maryland Court paid Thomas Brandson 2,000 lbs. of tobacco to keep the ferry.

Brick House Ferry   Pamunkey River. Noted on the plat of the town of West Point, Virginia, 1781.

Bruff's Ferry   Miles River. From Thomas Bruff's landing to Barrow's landing, Talbot County, Maryland. Received 6,000 lbs. of tobacco to operate. Later known as Miles River Ferry.

Bryan's Ferry   Chesapeake Bay. Broad Creek, Kent Island, Queen Anne's County, Maryland to Annapolis. John Bryan advertised good boats and hands in *Maryland Gazette*, December 31, 1767.

Budd's Ferry   Potomac River. From Goose Bay, Charles County, Maryland to Shipping Point, Virginia. Run by Mrs. Budd of Charles County, constantly watched by navy, which had cannon placed there during Civil War. Confederates had cannon on opposite shore.

Burgholder's Ferry   Susquehanna River. Two and one-half miles below Conestoga Creek, Maryland. Listed in report prepared for Gen. Charles Cornwallis, 1778.

Burwell's Ferry   James River. At Kingsmill Plantation, four miles from Williamsburg, used by George Washington. Also known as Hog Island Ferry.

Bush River Ferry   Bush River, Maryland. William Osborne got the land on the east side of the river in 1667 and built one of the first houses in the town of Old Baltimore and operated a ferry from his landing.

Cannon Ferry   Nanticoke River. Near Seaford, Sussex County, Delaware. Isaac and Elizabeth Cannon received a permit from the state to operate a ferry in 1793. Name changed to Woodland, 1882. Operated daily by the state of Delaware.

Canton Car Ferry   Baltimore Harbor. Operated by the Baltimore and Ohio Railroad to transfer freight and passenger cars from its Locust Point terminal to a slip at Third Avenue, 1886–1895.

Carren's Ferry   Bohemia River. John Carren advertised sailing ferry on Bohemia River going to any part of Virginia or Maryland, 1729.

Carter's Ferry   Corrotoman River. Operated by Thomas Carter probably before 1654. In that year he sold it to Major John Carter. Usually ran between Quiocomach to Ferry Point, Virginia; ceased operation in 1742.

Chancellor's Point Ferry   Northeast River. From Charlestown to Elk Neck, Cecil County, Maryland. Operated for about five years while Charlestown was the seat of justice, 1780s.

Chesapeake Bay Ferry Commission   Chesapeake Bay. Little Creek, Virginia to Kiptopeke on Virginia's Eastern Shore. 1954–1964, operated by the Commonwealth of Virginia.

Chesapeake Ferry Company   Hampton Roads. Old Point Comfort to Willoughby Spit. Organized 1912, double-ended auto ferry, replaced by bridge-tunnel 1957.

Choptank River Ferries   Caroline County, Maryland. Operated by the county. Melville's Warehouse to the west side of the river above Denton, Gilpin's Point, Price's Landing in Tuckahoe Neck, Hog Island to Talbot County. Ferry at Denton was free to residents.

Chownings Ferry   Rappahannock River. Begun by John Pine in 1702 from Dudleys Plantation to Chownings Point. Maintained until circa 1897.

Claiborne's Ferry   Pamunkey River. Sweet Hall, New Kent County, Virginia on main road to Williamsburg. Used by George Washington, became Ruffin's Ferry in 1769.

Claiborne–Annapolis Ferry Company   Chesapeake Bay. 1916 Maryland General Assembly authorized establishment of ferry from Annapolis to Claiborne, Talbot County. Eastern terminus changed to Matapeake, Kent Island, Queen Anne's County, 1930. Western terminus changed in 1941 to Sandy Point, Anne Arundel County. Ceased operation 1952.

Claremont–Sandy Point Ferry   James River. Auto and passenger ferry, listed as in operation in *Virginia, A Guide to the Old Dominion*, 1940.

Clifford's Ferry   Potomac River. John Clifford rented Hugh West's ferry in Alexandria, Virginia and in 1782 opened a tavern there.

Clifton's Neck Ferry   Potomac River. Fairfax County, Virginia to Frazier's Point, Prince Georges County, Maryland. Authorized by Virginia legislature, 1745, operated until 1808. Site of large, well-known springs near ferry house. Favorite area for picnics.

Coan–Bundick Ferry   Coan River. Northumberland County, Virginia, Coan Wharf to Bundick, one-car cable ferry, operated until 1934.

Collin's Ferry   Transquaking River. Dorchester County, Maryland.

Columbia Steam Ferry and Towboat Company   Susquehanna River. Between Wrightsville, Lancaster County and Columbia, York County, Pennsylvania. 1890–1924.

Conrad's Ferry   Potomac River. Near Poolesville, Montgomery County, Maryland to Loudon County, Virginia. Established circa 1828 by Earnest Conrad. Later known as White's Ferry. Operating in 2000.

Cresap's Ferry   Susquehanna River. Between Lapidum, Harford County and Port Deposit, Cecil County, Maryland. Established by Thomas Cresap, 1730.

Creswell's Ferry   Susquehanna River. Owned by Colonel John Creswell.

Crossharbor Ferry   Baltimore Harbor. Between Broadway, Fells Point and Haubert Street, Locust Point. Begun as Locust Point Ferry Co., 1851. Run by Baltimore City Harbor Board, 1915–1939.

Crotcher's Ferry   Marshyhope Creek, northwest fork of Nanticoke River, authorized by Maryland General Assembly, 1671.

Crouche's Ferry   Susquehanna River. Four and one-half miles below Postethwaite's Ferry. Listed in report prepared for Gen. Charles Cornwallis, 1778.

Dade's Ferry   Potomac River. Between Nanjemoy, Charles County, Maryland and Metomkin, Virginia, 1740s. Robert Dade advertised good boat and hands.

Dadler's Ferry   Mattaponi River. Shown on plat of town of West Point, Virginia, 1781. Used by George Washington.

Dansie's Ferry   Pamunkey River. King William County, Virginia. Operated by Thomas Dansie, who received his license in 1754 and also ran an ordinary. Often used by George Washington.

Deheniossa's Ferry   Patuxent River. Prince George's County to Anne Arundel County, operated by Alexander Deheniossa, who was also an innkeeper, in 1705.

Dent's Ferry   Potomac River. Persimmon Point, King George County, Virginia to Popes Creek, Charles County, Maryland. Operated by George Dent, 1740s, who advertised that his route avoided a dangerous creek used by other ferries and that the way to his ferry was well marked at convenient places.

Dixon's Ferry   Rappahannock River. Roger Dixon's land on Fredericksburg, Virginia waterfront to Stafford County. Used by George Washington.

Doncastle's Ferry   Pamunkey River. George Washington dined at the ordinary here on a trip to Williamsburg.

Doniphan Ferry   Rappahannock River. From the lands of Anderson Doniphan, King George County to those of Lawrence Battaile, Caroline County, 1755–1760.

Dorsey's Ferry   Patapsco River. Run by the Widow Dorsey, eighteenth century.

Dover Ferry   Choptank River. Authorized by 1671 Maryland General Assembly.

Downe's Ferry   Susquehanna River. Below Lowe's Ferry, also called Vinekar's Ferry, listed in report prepared for Gen. Charles Cornwallis, 1778.

Dudley's Ferry   York River. Noted by Benjamin H. Latrobe.

Edward's Ferry   Potomac River. Leesburg, Loudon County, Virginia to Montgomery County, Maryland. Used by the Army of the Potomac, 1863.

Elizabeth River Ferries   Elizabeth River. First ferry operated by Adam Thoroughgood 1636, continuous ferry service from then until tunnel opening, 1952. In 2000 commuter ferries operated by Tidewater Regional Transit (TRT).

Elk Ferry   Elk River. Near Elkton, Cecil County, Maryland. Mentioned by Dr. Alexander Hamilton during 1744 trip.

Eyre's Ferry   Chesapeake Bay. Littleton Eyre and family were authorized by Virginia General Assembly to operate from 1745 to 1770s. From Hungars Creek, Eastern Shore of Virginia to Norfolk, Hampton, Yorktown.

Faunteleroy's (Fauntleroy) Ferry   Rappahannock River. Landon Carter of Sabine Hall noted in his diary for March 25, 1712 that "Mr. Carter and Lady went over at Faunteleroy's Ferry."

Fendall's Ferry   Potomac River. Benjamin Fendall's landing, Charles County, Maryland goes to Hooe's Ferry, King George County, Virginia. Kept by James Nottingham, 1764, who also had a tavern. Used by George Washington.

Fitzhugh's Ferry   Potomac River. 1705, operated by Colonel William Fitzhugh from Stafford County, Virginia to Charles County, Maryland.

Floyd's Ferry   Chesapeake Bay. From Kings Creek, Eastern Shore of Virginia to Norfolk, Yorktown, Hampton. John K. Floyd got license to operate, 1822.

Foese's Ferry   Chickahominy River. Operated by John Foese, used by Thomas Jefferson June l, 1775. Former operators were Mary Davies and Robert Lorton who rented the ferry and ordinary which were on the Charles City County side of the river, 1769–1770. Called Lorton's 1770–1774, and Bryan's from 1776.

Foot's Ferry   Susquehanna River. Below Postethwaite's Ferry. Listed in report prepared for Gen. Charles Cornwallis, 1778.

Ford's Ferry   Rappahannock River. John Ford operated a ferry in 1686 from Cut Point Creek to Mount Landing Creek. Operated between two court houses: the day before, the day of, and the day after court.

Fox Ferry   Potomac River. From Oxon Creek, Prince Georges County, Maryland to Alexandria, Virginia. Leased by George Fox from the Berry family in the 1800s. This ferry, under various renters, was used as a smuggling base during the Civil War, and as base for corn and rye whiskey smuggling during Prohibition. Ceased operating circa 1932.

Frazier's Ferry   Mattaponi River. On Williamsburg road. Run by William Frazier. Frazier also operated a shipyard, built flat-bottomed boats for

Lafayette's army to use in the siege of Yorktown, 1781. Boats were to be large enough to carry 40 soldiers, but light enough to be drawn on carriages by only two horses.

Gibb's Ferry   Pocomoke River. Eastern Shore of Maryland. Abraham Gibbs was paid 2,500 pounds of tobacco in 1766 to operate a ferry on the upper river.

Glatz' Ferry   Susquehanna River. Another name for Anderson's Ferry.

Gloucester Point Ferry   York River. York County to Gloucester County, Virginia. Listed as in operation in *Virginia, A Guide to the Old Dominion*, 1940.

Gooch's Ferry   York River. Used by George Washington.

Goodman's Ferry   Chesapeake Bay. Broad Creek, Kent Island, Queen Anne's County, Maryland to Annapolis. Richard Goodman advertised good boats and skillful hands in *Maryland Gazette*, 1761.

Goose Creek Ferry   Goose Creek. Near Hough's Mill, Loudon County, Virginia. George Washington was obliged to use it March 13, 1771 because freshet made fording impossible.

Great Wicomico Ferry   Wicomico River, Northern Neck of Virginia, Tipers to Blackwells Wharf. Established 1895, operated by Oliver Christian in 1892, by L. R. Headley in 1901. Discontinued 1936.

Grey's Point Ferry   Rappahannock River. White Stone Wharf, Lancaster County, Virginia to Greys Point, Middlesex County. A 60-foot diesel ferry operated here 1927–1957.

Griffin & Wheatly Ferry   Potomac River. Leased Fox–Berry Ferry in 1860s and ran small, passenger-only ferries, to and from Alexandria, Virginia.

Griffith's Ferry   Fishing Creek. To Hooper's Island, Maryland. Operated by John Griffith in 1786 for 15 pounds salary. Griffith's boat carried 4 men and 4 horses.

Grigg's Ferry   Patuxent River. 1676 John Grigg and his assignees were authorized to keep a ferry from his house to the opposite plantation, Maryland.

Hackley's Ferry   Rappahannock River. Begun 1732 by John T. Hackley, taken over by widow Judith, 1760, from Gawen Corbin's Moss Neck property in Caroline County to Richard Corbin's Farleyvale Plantation.

Hall's Ferry   Corrotoman River. Shown on 1826 map of the western branch of the river, Northern Neck of Virginia.

Hamilton's Ferry   Potomac River. William Hamilton ran ferry from his place at Metomkin to Riverside, Charles County, Maryland, 1813.

Hammit's Ferry   Monocacy River. Robert Hammit, Frederick County, fined for lack of license to operate ferry, 1787.

Hammond's Ferry   Breton Bay. John Hammond was licensed in 1654 to operate a ferry across the bay, St. Mary's County, Maryland.

Hampton Roads Transportation Company   Hampton Roads. Organized in 1925, ferries from Old Point Comfort to Willoughby spit. Company absorbed by Chesapeake Ferry Company, 1929.

Harper's Ferry   Above junction of Potomac and Shenandoah Rivers.

Licensed to Robert Harper 1734. Now site of town of Harper's Ferry, West Virginia.

Harris' Ferry Wicomico River. 1658 Samuel Harris was licensed by Charles County, Maryland court to operate a ferry.

Harris' Ferry Susquehanna River. Begun in 1753 by John Harris (1726–1791). Now site of Harrisburg, Pennsylvania.

Harrison's Ferry Potomac River. Richard Harrison was authorized to operate ferry by Virginia Assembly in 1744. Between Nanjemoy, Maryland and Metomkin, Virginia.

Hawkin's Ferry Potomac River, Prince George's County, Maryland to Fairfax County, Virginia. Prince George's County Court issued a license for the ferry in March 1782 to George Frazier Hawkins and Matthew Wigfield; in Sept. 1788 to William Baylew; and in 1795 again to Matthew Wigfield.

Hawley's Ferry Southampton River, Virginia. Henry Hawley received a patent from the colony for this ferry in 1640. Patent provided for a life monopoly if he did not charge more than one penny for a passenger.

Hickman's Ferry Used by George Washington.

Hog Island Ferry James River. Surrey County to James City County, Virginia a few miles below Jamestown. Used by George Washington. Also known as Burwell's Ferry.

Hooe's Ferry Potomac River. Mathias Point, King George County, Virginia to Cedar Point, Charles County, Maryland. Main north-south link through the tidewater, Annapolis to Williamsburg. Begun 1720, continued into late nineteenth century.

Hopewell–Charles City Ferry James River. Listed as in operation in *Virginia, A Guide to the Old Dominion*, 1940.

Hopkinson's Ferry Tred Avon River. Long Point to Island Point to Mr. Phil Stevenson's point, Talbot County, Maryland. Run by Jonathan Hopkinson, 1668–1672, carrying passengers and horses. 1671 County Levy paid him 2,500 lbs. of tobacco yearly.

Hungars Creek Ferry Chesapeake Bay. Twice weekly from Northampton County, Virginia to Yorktown and Hampton. Begun 1705.

Hunter's Ferry Rappahannock River. In King George County, operated by James Hunter in 1755, George Washington noted that he lent him a small sum of money.

Hutching's Ferry Chesapeake Bay. Kent Island, Queen Anne's County, Maryland to Annapolis. Operated by James Hutchings who petitions for a public road to his home in 1751. Advertised the ferry in 1766, also kept a tavern. In 1802 Kitty Hutching kept the ferry, using one large boat.

Iiam's Ferry South River. Near Londontown, Anne Arundel County, Maryland to Annapolis. Samuel Iiams fined three pounds April 8, 1786 for leaving ferry unattended.

Irvington–Grey's Point Ferry Rappahannock River. Linked Northern Neck of Virginia with the Middle Peninsula, listed as in operation in *Virginia, A Guide to the Old Dominion*, 1940.

Island Ferry Whitehouse Creek. Northern Neck of Virginia from Brown's Plantation to "the island where John Pyne lives." Authorized 1657, ran about three years. In his diary for April 25, 1766 Landon Carter mentions an Island Ferry, but gives no identification.

Jamestown Ferry James River. From Jamestown, Virginia to Scotland, Surrey County. Begun 1925, operated by Virginia Department of Transportation since 1945.

Jawert's Ferry Elk River. Between Elk Neck and Court House Point, Cecil County, Maryland. 1720 John Jawert lost license for letting slaves run the ferry. Herman Kinkey, tavern keeper, was appointed to replace him.

Johnson's Ferry Susquehanna River. Cecil County, Maryland. Listed in the report prepared for Gen. Charles Cornwallis, 1778.

Johnson's Ferry Potomac River. Above Mt. Vernon, Virginia. Famous for springs, George Washington attended boat races and barbeques there.

Jone's Ferry Chesapeake Bay. Richard I. Jones was licensed in 1811 by the Queen Anne's County Levy Court to ferry passengers to Anne Arundel County. He charged $1 each if more than one was crossing. He also had a fast packet sailing sloop, *Caroline*, which accommodated passengers, horses, and carriages.

Jones' Ferry Potomac River. Lower Cedar Point, Charles County, Maryland to King George County, Virginia. Charles Jones advertised his ferry as the nearest way to Williamsburg, 1740s.

Keene's Ferry Patuxent River. Calvert County, Maryland. Richard Keene replaced George Beckworth as ferryman, 1675.

King's Creek Ferry Chesapeake Bay. From Northampton County, Virginia to Yorktown, York County, Virginia. Operated until 1724

Laidler's Ferry Potomac River. Lower Cedar Point, Charles County, Maryland to Hooe's Ferry, King George County, Virginia. John Laidler advertised in *Maryland Gazette*, 1763. Discontinued 1847. Also spelled "Laidlaws."

Layton's Ferry Rappahannock River. About twenty miles above Tappahannock, Essex County, Virginia on the south side of river, opposite Leedstown Ferry, eighteenth century.

Leedstown Ferry Rappahannock River. About twenty miles above Tappahannock, Essex County, Virginia on the north side of river, opposite Layton's Ferry, in eighteenth century on preferred stage route Annapolis to Williamsburg. Discontinued 1927.

Level–Green–Essex Ferry Rappahannock River. Near Wellford, Richmond County, Virginia to Essex County. Begun by Bladen Hall after the Civil War.

Little Ferry Upper Machodoc Creek. Northern Neck of Virginia, about where Route 218 crosses creek. In use until 1907, a forty-foot span crossed by a rowboat.

Little Wicomico River Ferry Established by Northumberland County, Virginia in 1906.

Lodge Ferry Lodge Creek. Across the mouth of Lodge Creek, Northumberland County, Virginia. From the public landing at Lodge to Cherry Point. Begun 1913, discontinued 1919.

Londontown Ferry   South River. Londontown, Anne Arundel County, Maryland, made a port of entry 1683, several ferries in vicinity across river to Annapolis. On main route Philadelphia to Williamsburg. Ferrymen included William T. Green, DeWise Boyer (1821–1825), Benjamin Pinale, Jacob H. Slemaher, James Larimore, and William Brown, who advertised himself also as a joiner, cabinetmaker in 1772.

Lovell's Ferry   Potomac River. From Lower Cedar Point, Charles County, Maryland to White Point (site of Colonial Beach), Westmoreland County, Virginia. Operated by Robert Lovell, 1734–1764.

Lowe's Ferry   Susquehanna River. Three miles below Rankin's Ferry. Listed in report prepared for Gen. Charles Cornwallis, 1778.

Lower Ferry   Susquehanna River. Between Perryville, Cecil County and Havre de Grace, Harford County, Maryland. Begun 1695 by Jacob Young and William York, important crossing on main East-West post road, Philadelphia to Baltimore. Used by the Philadelphia, Wilmington and Baltimore Railroad from 1837–1866.

Lower Ferry   Rappahannock River. Often used by George Washington, opposite his mother's home, Fredericksburg, Virginia. Noted October 22, 1772 that he paid a year and three months' ferriage, 12s/6d.

Luney's Ferry   James River. Used by George Washington.

Mackubbin's Ferry   South River, Maryland. R. MacKubbin kept a ferry over the South River above Londontown and advertised that his was a shorter and easier route to Annapolis than the Londontown Ferry.

Magruder's Ferry   Patuxent River. Prince George's County, Maryland. Prince George's County Court issued a license for the ferry to Henry Compton in April 1795, and in March 1782 to Isaac Rollings.

Manhasset Ferry   Elizabeth River, Virginia. Nicknamed the "Nanny Ferry," used by commuters between Norfolk and Portsmouth in the 1870s.

Maryland, Delaware, and Virginia Railway Company   Chesapeake Bay. Ferry connected railroad in Baltimore with that in Queenstown, then Love Point, Queen Anne's County, Maryland. Early twentieth century.

Mason's Ferry   Occoquan River. Fairfax County to Woodbridge, Prince William County, Virginia, about ten miles south of Mt. Vernon, Virginia. Established by Virginia General Assembly 1681. Operated by George Mason's family. This was on a main North-South route. Bridge built 1795. Mason also ran a ferry across the Potomac River at Rock Creek in Maryland.

Master's Ferry   Chesapeake Bay. 1724 John Masters gave bond to run ferry on Eastern Shore of Virginia (Hungars Creek) to Yorktown and Hampton.

Mattox Ferry   Mattox Creek. Westmoreland County, Virginia about one-fourth of a mile above present bridge. Begun 1697, bridge built 1754. Subsidized by county in eighteenth century to insure dependable service for passengers going to Appomattox Church on Sunday.

Maxwell's Ferry Patapsco River. County court appointed James Maxwell to keep a ferry to and from Stoney Barr at the town of Joppa, 1713. Town declined in early 1800s. Ferry landing owned by Widow Adams.

McCall's Ferry Susquehanna River. Below Reed's Ferry, listed in report prepared for Gen. Charles Cornwallis, 1778.

Merry Point Ferry Corrotoman River. Lancaster County, Virginia, Merry Point to Ottoman Wharf, established 1873, closed as of this printing.

Middle Ferry Susquehanna River. Below Peach Bottom Ferry, listed in report prepared for Gen. Charles Cornwallis, 1778.

Middleton's Ferry Chesapeake Bay. Annapolis to Kent Island, Queen Anne's County and Rock Hall, Kent County, Maryland. Samuel Middleton advertised in *Maryland Gazette*, 1751, also kept important tavern at Annapolis dock.

Monaskon Ferry Rappahannock River. From Monaskon plantation house to Waterview Wharf, Essex County, Virginia. Begun 1744, ran for twenty-nine years.

Mount Pleasant Ferry Patuxent River. Prince George's County Court issued a license for the ferry in March 1784 to Bartholomew Bromley and in April 1822 to Henry Waring.

New York, Philadelphia, and Norfolk Railroad Chesapeake Bay. Operated ferry for train connection, Cape Charles, Northampton County, Virginia to Old Point Comfort, Norfolk, 1885–1953.

Nicols' Ferry James River. From Deborah N. Barker's landing to Hog Island, Virginia. Nicols paid 4,000 lbs. of tobacco to operate in 1760. Sum to be reduced if there were not sufficient hands or boats.

Nobletz' Ferry Susquehanna River. Listed in report prepared for Gen. Charles Cornwallis, 1778.

Noland's Ferry Potomac River. Used by George Washington.

Nominy Ferry Landon Carter notes in his diary, Nov. 15, 1770, that he sent his tumbrel to Blaine's Store via the ferry to pick up cotton he had bought.

Norfolk and Atlantic Terminal Company Hampton Roads. Pine Beach, Norfolk to Old Point Comfort and Newport News, early 1900s.

Norwood's Ferry Severn River. Joseph Norwood received license in 1682 to operate ferry over Severn. Petition says he has several conveniences there to keep a ferry.

Nottingham Ferry Patuxent River. Prince George's County Court issued a license in Sept. 1788 to Edward Griffiths to operate this ferry; in April 1818 to Henry Boswell and William G. Jackson, and in April 1834 to John Calvert and Robert M. Tomlin.

Osborne's Ferry Bush River. Old House Point, Harford County, Maryland settled by ferryman William Osborne in 1667.

Oxford-Bellevue Ferry Tred Avon River. Talbot County, Maryland. Authorized by Talbot County Court 1683, still in operation.

Oxon Ferry Potomac River, Prince George's County, Maryland to Fairfax

County, Virginia. Prince George's County Court issued a license for this ferry in April 1795 to Joseph Thomas.

Parker's Ferry Chesapeake Bay. Pungoteague Creek, Accomack County, Virginia to Yorktown, Hampton, Norfolk. Henry Parker licensed as ferryman in 1814.

Patapsco Ferry Patapsco River. Baltimore County, Maryland, Council of Safety paid Widow Dorsey to operate in 1777. George Washington used the ferry May 7, 1775, ferriage 6s/6d.

Patuxent Ferry Patuxent River. Mentioned twice by Philip Vickers Fithian, "a small ferry," Oct. 22, 1774, April 13, 1774. Also from Millstone Landing, St. Mary's County to Solomons, Calvert County, Maryland ferrying cars and passengers, 1930s.

Peach Bottom Ferry Susquehanna River. Listed in report prepared for Gen Charles Cornwallis, 1778.

Peninsula Ferry Company Chesapeake Bay, Pine Beach, Norfolk to Cape Charles, Northampton County, Virginia. Discontinued March 31, 1933.

Perkins' Ferry Susquehanna River. Lapidum, Harford County to Port Deposit, Cecil County, Maryland. Formerly Cresap's Ferry, owned from 1733 to 1772 by William and Reuben Perkins.

Philadelphia, Wilmington and Baltimore Railroad Company Susquehanna River. 1838–1866 used steam ferries to transport passengers and rail cars across at the river's mouth, Cecil County to Harford County, Maryland.

Plant Patch Ferry Cat Point Creek, formerly Rappahannock Creek, Northern Neck of Virginia. Authorized by county court in 1859 when a storm washed out the bridge. Used until a new bridge built in 1887.

Port Tobacco Ferry Port Tobacco River. Charles County, Maryland. Well-traveled route in colonial era.

Posey's Ferry Potomac River. Next to Mt. Vernon, Fairfax County, Virginia to land of Thomas Wallis, Prince George's County, Maryland. Authorized by legislature 1745 and owned by John Posey; owned by George Washington, 1772.

Postethwaite's Ferry Susquehanna River. Pennsylvania. First ferry below Taff's listed in report prepared for Gen. Charles Cornwallis, 1778.

Potomac Beach–Morgantown Ferry Potomac River. Carried buses of the Peninsula Bus Line and as many as 35 cars across the river between Virginia and Maryland. Operated until 1934.

Potomac Ferry Company Potomac River. Added steamboat *Wawaset* in 1865. On a crowded trip, August 8, 1873, the ferry burst into flames mid-river and 76 people perished.

Potomac Ferry And Transportation Company Potomac River. Begun 1919 McGuire's Wharf, Nomini Creek, Westmoreland County, Virginia to Leonardtown, St. Mary's County, Maryland. Also known as Whiskey Ferry.

Queen Anne's Ferry & Equipment Company Chesapeake Bay and Chester River. Baltimore to Queenstown, Queen Anne's County, 1894–1905, connected with train for shore points.

Quimby's Ferry   Chester River. Ann Quimby kept ferry from Kingstown, Queen Anne's County to Chestertown, Kent County, Maryland, 1815.

Rankin's Ferry, Susquehanna River   Below falls, past Conowingo Creek, Cecil County, Maryland. Listed in report prepared for Gen. Charles Cornwallis, 1778.

Reed's Ferry   Susquehanna River. Below Burgholder's. Listed in report prepared for Gen. Charles Cornwallis, 1778.

Richmond–Eastern Shore Ferry Company   Chesapeake Bay. Established 1933, auto, truck, passenger steam ferry from Deltaville, Middlesex County to Harborton, Accomack County, Virginia. Ran for two years.

Ritchie's Ferry   Rappahannock River. Established 1764. Essex County to Richmond County, Virginia. Also known as Richmond Courthouse Ferry, Warsaw Ferry, Island Ferry, Crandall's Ferry, Brockenbrough's Ferry. Bridge built 1927.

Robert's Ferry   Chesapeake Bay. Elias Roberts and Michael Christian gave bond in 1731 to run ferry from Hungars Creek on Virginia's Eastern Shore to Yorktown and Hampton.

Rock Creek Ferry   Rock Creek. District of Columbia to Arlington County, Virginia. Owned by George Mason in eighteenth century. Used until late nineteenth century.

Rock Run's Ferry   Susquehanna River. Below Peach Bottom Ferry, listed in report prepared for Gen. Charles Cornwallis, 1778.

Rockett's Ferry   James River. Near Richmond, Virginia. Robert Rockett had ferry about 1730; mentioned and sketched by Benjamin H. Latrobe.

Roy's Ferry   Rappahannock River. John Roy established a warehouse and ferry at site of Port Royal in 1725. Ran from Caroline County to King George County, Virginia until 1776.

Ruffin's Ferry   Pamunkey River. New Kent County, Virginia. George Washington stopped here April 30, 1771 to tend sick horse; he often used this ferry. Formerly Claiborne's Ferry, bought by Robert Ruffin, 1769. River bridge 1926.

Sassafras Ferry   Sassafras River. Kent County to Cecil County, Maryland, used by Dr. Alexander Hamilton during 1744 trip. A 1736 assembly bill had voted to erect a town on the tract owned by Gideon Pearce called "Tolchester" at the place where the ferry was kept.

Seal's Ferry   Rappahannock River. Hayfield Wharf to Conway's Warehouse, begun in 1730 by Anthony Seals, ceased operating 1815.

Severn River Ferry   Severn River. Anne Arundel County, Maryland (various Annapolis locations: Joyce Lane, Severn Avenue, Ferry Point at foot of Maryland Avenue, Whitney's Landing to Spa Creek, Dorsey's Creek). In March 1694 Captain John Hamond and Major Edward Dorsey were licensed to keep ferries as cheaply as possible over the Severn River. During ensuing years ferries were operated by many persons, including Joseph Norwood 1682, Allen Robinett 1695, Roger B. White 1695, Henry

Duval 1821–1822, Mary Duval 1823–1833, Jonathan Selby 1825–1826, Mary Selby 1823–1833, George Hayden 1834–1837, Zachariah Duvall 1834–1835, and Anne Arundel County until 1887. In the early twentieth century Henry Keidel ran a ferry across the river; every July 4th he would position it full of fireworks in the middle of the river and give the citizens a patriotic show.

Sharptown Ferry   Nanticoke River. Thirty miles up the river at the northern-most corner of Wicomico County; closed in 1909 when a bridge was built.

Smith's Ferry   Susquehanna River. Lapidum, Harford County to Port Deposit, Cecil County, Maryland. Formerly Perkins' Ferry, bought by Thomas Smith 1772, kept by his sons until 1793.

South River Ferries   There were many ferries over the South River, especially in the vicinity of Londontown which crossing to Annapolis was one of the main North-South routes in colonial times. In March 1776 Colonel John Weems was ordered to station half of his battalion on one side of the river and the other half on the opposite side so that if a man-of-war and its tender came up the river they could be repelled.

Southin's Ferry   Rappahannock River. Naylors to Tappahannock, Essex County, Virginia. Operated late 1670s–1778 by order of court to take people to church and court. Used by George Washington, 1760.

Speake's Ferry   Potomac River. Lawson Speakes fined five pounds in 1788 for keeping ferry without a license. Charles County, Maryland.

Spooner's Ferry   Potomac River. Cedar Point, Charles County, Maryland to Westmoreland County, Virginia. G. W. Spooner advertised in *Maryland Gazette*, Tuesday, February 20, 1766: "This is to give notice that the subscriber has a new erected FERRY on Patawmack River in Virginia, opposite to Cedar Point in Maryland, 24 miles distant from Westmoreland Court House, 40 from Richmond, 12 from King George, 26 from Stafford, from Leeds Town 15 miles, from Port Royal 12 and from Fredericksburg 34 miles. There is a good Ferry kept with Entertainment." Spooner kept the ferry from 1764 until the Revolutionary War period.

Stevens' Ferry   Lower Pocomoke River. Pocomoke City, Worcester County, Maryland. Established by Colonel William Stevens, 1687. Mary Stevens, ferryman, paid 2,500 pounds of tobacco to run lower ferry in 1766.

Stevenson's Ferry   Susquehanna River. Another name for Susquehanna Lower Ferry.

Strother's Ferry   Rappahannock River. Anthony Strother's Landing in King George County, Virginia to public lot in Fredericksburg. Advertised in *Virginia Gazette*, 1745. 1746 run by William Lynn and Archibald McPherson.

Sunnybank Ferry   Little Wicomico River. Northumberland County, Virginia at Route 644. Authorized by assembly in 1906, in 2000 operated by Virginia Department of Transportation.

Sutton's Ferry   Chesapeake Bay. Ashbury Sutton, Annapolis shipbuilder, kept a ferry from Annapolis to Kent Island, Maryland, 1746.

Swearington's Ferry Potomac River. Shepherdstown, West Virginia to Frederick, Maryland. Run by Thomas Swearington. Used by George Washington, General Edward Braddock, 1755.

Taff's Ferry Susquehanna River. First ferry below Harris' Ferry. Listed in report prepared for Gen. Charles Cornwallis, 1778.

Taliaferro Ferry Rappahannock River. Established by Francis L. Taliaferro in 1742 from his warehouse and wharf at mouth of Mill Creek, one and one-half miles below Port Royal, Virginia. Widow Mary Taliaferro operated until late 1770s.

Tankersley's Ferry Rappahannock River. At Port Royal, Virginia. Authorized 1722, operated for 36 years. Landon Carter notes in his diary, March 18, 1752, that the Virginia Assembly passed a bill for a free ferry at Port Royal; he does not give a name.

Thompson's Ferry Potomac River. Lower Cedar Point, Charles County, Maryland to Potomac Beach, Westmoreland County, Virginia, operated by Henry Thompson, rival of nearby ferrymen, Robert Dade, Richard Harrison, George Dent, and Charles Jones, mid-eighteenth century. Thompson advertised that he had a fine "Yawl" if a passenger did not wish to ride with his horses. He also was building a ferryboat large enough to hold six horses.

Thoroughgood's Ferry Elizabeth River. Norfolk to Portsmouth, Virginia. Adam Thoroughgood authorized to operate in 1636.

Tidewater Regional Transit Elizabeth River. Commuter ferries Norfolk to Portsmouth.

Tidewater Transportation Company Hampton Roads. From Newport News to Norfolk, Virginia, organized 1900.

Toot's Ferry Susquehanna River. Listed in report prepared for Gen. Charles Cornwallis, 1778.

Totuskey Ferry Totuskey Creek. Circhmond County, Virginia circa 1689, first bridge built 1742.

Traver's Ferry Slaughter Creek, Dorchester County, Maryland. Henry Travers advertised gaily painted sailing ferry; widow Elizabeth authorized by court to take over in 1786.

Tubman's Ferry Tar Bay, Dorchester County, Maryland to mouth of Patuxent River. County court issued a license for the ferry in 1787 to Richard Tubman with yearly pay of 50 pounds. Ferriage for a four-wheel carriage was ld, 15s.

Tucker's Ferry West River and Chesapeake Bay. West River, Anne Arundel County to Kent Island, Queen Anne's County, Talbot County, or Dorchester County, Maryland. Sele Tucker advertised in *Maryland Gazette*, Sept. 27, 1773.

Tyler's Ferry Potomac River. South of Lower Machodoc Creek, Virginia to Cedar Point, Maryland. William Tyler authorized to run in 1759. Used by Philip Vickers Fithian in April and October 1774.

Upper Ferry Nomini Creek. Virginia. 1696–1887. Eighteenth century used by clergy and parishioners going to Nomini Church.

Upper Ferry Wicomico River. Wicomico County, Maryland, about six miles below Salisbury. Begun late eighteenth century, still in operation.

Utie's Ferry Chesapeake Bay. From Nathaniel Utie's home on Spesutia Island to mainland, Harford County, Maryland. 1658–1900s.

Varina Ferry James River. From Henrico County to Chesterfield County, about 12 miles SE of Richmond. Used by Thomas Jefferson.

Vienna Ferry Nanticoke River. Dorchester County to Wicomico County, Maryland. Established 1706.

Vinekar's Ferry Susquehanna River. Below Lowe's Ferry, also known as Downs' Ferry, listed in report prepared for Gen. Charles Cornwallis, 1778.

Virginia Ferry Corporation Chesapeake Bay. Little Creek to Cape Charles, Northampton County, Virginia. Begun April 1, 1933. Acquired by Commonwealth of Virginia, 1956, and named Chesapeake Bay Ferry Commission.

Ward's Ferry Chesapeake Bay. Kings Creek, Eastern Shore of Virginia to Norfolk, Hampton. 1634 court order gave William Ward, ferryman, power to attach property of those not paying ferriage.

Ware's Ferry Rappahannock River. Dunnsville to Wellord's Wharf, Northern Neck of Virginia. Begun 1751, well known as dependable and safe, ran for 176 years. Advertised auto ferry in 1922.

Watkins' Ferry Potomac River. Pole ferry operated by Evan Watkins where Great Wagon Road crossed river; authorized by Virginia Assembly, 1744.

West's Ferry Potomac River. Hugh West received a license in 1744 to operate a ferry from his landing at the foot of Oronoco St., Alexandria, Virginia to Frazier's Point, Oxon Hill, Maryland.

White's Ferry Potomac River. Montgomery County, Maryland to Loudon County, Virginia. Formerly Conrad's Ferry. Established circa 1828; still in operation.

White Rock Hall Ferry Chesapeake Bay. Operated by James Hodges from Rock Hall, Maryland to Annapolis. He also kept a ferry house. Thomas Jefferson noted using this ferry, August 3, 1775.

Whitehaven Ferry Wicomico River. Somerset County to Wicomico County, Maryland. Below Salisbury. Begun late seventeenth century; still in operation.

Whiting's Ferry Rappahannock River. Begun by Ralph Whiting about 1690, received authorization in1705. Three miles below Port Royal, Virginia, a semi-private plantation ferry between Woodlawn and Camden Plantations. Ceased 1745.

Williams' Ferry Pamunkey River. New Kent County to King William County, Virginia, near Custis Plantation at Claiborne's. Used by George Washington.

Wilson's Ferry Chesapeake Bay. Elizabeth Wilson operated deceased husband's ferry between Annapolis and Broad Creek, Kent Island, Maryland in the 1740s.

Woodland Ferry   Nanticoke River. Road 78, Sussex County, Delaware. Begun by Isaac and Elizabeth Cannon, 1793, still in operation. Formerly known as Cannon's Ferry.

Wright's Ferry   Susquehanna River. Between Columbia, Lancaster County and Wrightsville, York County, Pennsylvania. Established by John Wright 1730. Important crossing on Great Wagon Road.

Young's Ferry   Port Tobacco River. Charles County, Maryland. During Revolutionary War, site plundered by armed British soldiers when their schooners landed in area. Operated in 1781 by Mrs. Young.

Notes

CHAPTER 1. Settlement and Growth in the Virginia Tidewater

1. Arthur Pierce Middleton, *Tobacco Coast: A Maritime History of Chesapeake Bay in the Colonial Era* (Baltimore: Johns Hopkins University Press, 1984), 39.

2. Clarence Lee Beebe, "A History of the Chesapeake Bay Ferries to Virginia's Eastern Shore Prior to the Civil War" (master's thesis, University of Richmond, 1954), 7.

3. Paul Wilstach, *Tidewater Virginia* (Indianapolis: Bobbs-Merrill Company,1931), 102.

4. Matthew Page Andrews, *Virginia: The Old Dominion* (Garden City, NY: Doubleday, Doran, and Company, 1937), 35.

5. Philip L. Barbour, *The Complete Works of Captain John Smith (1580–1631),* Vol.1 (Boston: Houghton Mifflin Company, 1964), 225.

6. Regina Combs Hammett, *History of St. Mary's County, Maryland* (Leonardtown, MD: St. Mary's County Bicentennial Commission, 1977), 20.

7. James R. Perry, *The Formation of a Society on Virginia's Eastern Shore, 1615–1655* (Chapel Hill: University of North Carolina Press, 1990), 15.

8. According to Frederick Tilp, *The Chesapeake Bay of Yore, Mainly about Rowing and Sailing Craft,* (Annapolis: Chesapeake Bay Foundation, 1982), scows were flat-bottomed and at first propelled by poling or rowing. A

sloop had a round bottom, a keel up to 60 ft. in length, with one mast. Small schooners had two masts with a fore and aft rig, were shallow keeled, and had a round stem.

9. Benjamin Henry Latrobe, American architect, wrote and made sketches of his travels throughout the country. He often used ferries or made sketches of them, as well as the towns they were near, or the men who operated them. See Edwin C. Carter III, John C. Van Horne, and Charles E. Brownell, eds., *Latrobe's View of America, 1795–1820,* (New Haven: Yale University Press, 1985) 244, 245.

10. Clarence Lee Beebe, *A History of the Chesapeake Bay Ferries,* 7.

11. Adam Thoroughgood's ferry, established in 1636, is often referred to as the first on record. However, William Ward had court authorization for his ferry on Virginia's Eastern Shore in 1634, according to Clarence Lee Beebe.

12. John W. Reps, *Tidewater Towns: City Planning in Colonial Virginia and Maryland,* (Williamsburg: Colonial Williamsburg Foundation, 1972) 52.

13. Ibid., 80.

14. Ibid., 220.

15. Ibid., 116.

16. Ibid., 143.

CHAPTER 2. Emergence of a Ferry System in Virginia

1. Arthur Pierce Middleton, *Tobacco Coast,* 74, states that the Virginia Assembly passed acts in 1641 and 1643 creating free ferries paid for by county levy. In her *Some Notes on Shipbuilding and Shipping in Colonial Virginia,* 38, Cerinda W. Evans gives the year as 1642. Clarence Lee Beebe's *A History of the Chesapeake Ferries,* gives the date as 1641. All sources agree that the law was repealed after several years.

2. Clifford C. Presnall, "Ferries on the Northern Neck of Virginia," *Northern Neck of Virginia Historical Magazine* (1979): 3278. The longest running ferry was the Little Ferry, 1740–1970. The ferry that ran the briefest period of time, Dade's, Dent's, and Thompson's Ferries, only ran for about three years in the 1740s.

3. Clarence Lee Beebe, *A History of the Chesapeake Bay Ferries,* 21.

4. Ibid., 27.

5. Norma Miller Turman, *The Eastern Shore of Virginia, 1603–1964* (Onancock, VA: Eastern Shore News, 1964) 165.

CHAPTER 3. Potomac River Ferries

1. Paul Wilstach, *Potomac Landings* (New York: Tudor Publishing Co., 1937), 298.

2. Stanton, Richard L., *Potomac Journey: Fairfax Stone to Tidewater* (Washington, DC: Smithsonian Institution Press, 1993), 29.

3. W. W. Abbot and Dorothy Twohig, eds., *The Papers of George Washington, Colonial Series*, Vols. 1,7,8,9 (Charlottesville: University Press of Virginia, 1994), 296.

4. Paul Wilstach, *Tidewater Virginia*, 296.

5. Eric Mills, *Chesapeake Bay in the Civil War* (Centreville, MD: Tidewater Publishers, 1996), 57–58.

6. Kate Mason Rowland, *The Life of George Mason, 1752–1792, Vol. II* (New York: G. P. Putnam's Sons, 1892), 456.

7. T. Michael Miller, "Ferries," [n.p., n.d., lecture series] 26.

CHAPTER 4. Other Virginia Ferries

1. John W. Reps, *Tidewater Towns*, 70.

2. Tennyson Evans Hammack, "The Sunny Bank Ferry," *The Bulletin of the Northumberland Co. Historical Society* 21 (December 1984).

CHAPTER 5. Development of a Ferry System in Maryland

1. J. Hall Pleasants, ed., *Archives of Maryland, LIII, Proceedings of the County Court of Charles County, 1658–1666*, (1936): 53.

2. Ibid., 560.

3. J. Hall Pleasants, ed., *Archives of Maryland, L, Proceedings and Acts of the General Assembly of Maryland, 1752–1756*, (1933): 319.

4. The 1766 tax levy for Worcester, Co., Maryland lists payment of 1,500 pounds of tobacco to Jacob Cannon for keeping the ferry over the Nanticoke River. At that time Sussex County, Delaware was part of Worcester County. One can surmise that this Jacob Cannon is of the same family as Isaac and Elizabeth, who got a ferry license from Delaware in 1793. The Worcester County levy is listed in J. Hall Pleasants, ed., *Archives of Maryland, LXI, Proceedings and Acts of the General Assembly of Maryland, 1766–1768*, (1944): 505–10.

5. Ted Giles, *Patty Cannon, Woman of Mystery* (Easton, MD: Easton Publishing Co., 1965), 40, 70.

6. Aubrey C. Land, ed., *Archives of Maryland, LXXI, Journal and Correspondence of the State Council of Maryland 1784–1789* (1970): 218, 236.

7. Bernard Christian Steiner, ed., *Archives of Maryland, XLII, Proceedings and Acts of the General Assembly of Maryland*, (1923): 220.

8. Aubrey C. Land, ed., *Archives of Maryland, LXXI*, (1970): 26.

9. John Jawert kept a ferry across the Elk River. In 1720 citizens had him removed for mismanagement, i.e., letting his slaves run the ferry. George Johnston, *History of Cecil County, Maryland* (Elkton, MD: Genealogical Publishing Co., 1881) 189.

10. Donald Jackson and Dorothy Twohig, eds., *The Diaries of George Washington, Vol. VI, January 1790–December 1799* (Charlottesville: University Press of Virginia, 1979), 100–101.

11. Mary Ball Washington moved to Fredericksburg, Virginia in 1772. Prior to that she lived on a farm on the opposite side of the Rappahannock River.

12. Lockwood Barr, "William Faris, 1728–1804," *Maryland Historical Magazine* 36 (Decenber 1941): 420–39.

13. Philip Vickers Fithian, a Princeton graduate preparing for the Presbyterian ministry, spent a year (1773–1774) as tutor to the children of Robert Carter III at Nomini Hall, on the Northern Neck of Virginia. His copious diary gives much information of daily life and travel. Hunter Dickinson Farish ed., *Journal and Letters of Philip Vickers Fithian, 1773–1774: A Plantation Tutor of the Old Dominion* (Williamsburg: Colonial Williamsburg, Inc., 1943), 144, 274.

14. Frederic Emory, *Queen Anne's County, Maryland: Its Early History and Development,* (Baltimore: Maryland Historical Society) 1950, 57.

15. Hunter Dickinson Farish, ed., *Journal and Letters of Philip Vickers Fithian*, 146.

16. Isaac Weld Jr. was an Irish country gentleman who spent two years, 1795–1796, traveling throughout the United States. He kept a diary of his unfavorable impressions of the new country. G. E. Gifford Jr., ed. *Cecil County, Maryland: 1608–1850* (Rising Sun, MD: n.p., 1974), 121.

17. Ibid., 128.

18. John Blackford, *Diary: 1829*, n.c., n.p., n.d.

CHAPTER 6. Middle Bay Ferry Crossings

1. *The State of Maryland Historical Atlas* (State of Maryland, Department of Economic and Community Development), December 1973, 40.

2. William Hand Browne, ed., *Archives of Maryland, XXVI, Proceedings and Acts of the General Assembly of Maryland, Sept. 1704–April 1706* (1906): 250.

3. *Anne Arundel County Levy Book*. Annapolis: n.p., 1811–1836.

4. Arthur Pierce Middleton, *Tobacco Coast*, 72.

5. James A. Bear Jr. and Lucia C. Stanton, *The Papers of Thomas Jefferson, Second Series: Jefferson's Memorandum Books* (Princeton: Princeton University Press, 1997), 548.

6. Although the colonial ferry route from Rock Hall to Annapolis was one of the most important, there does not seem to be historic identification of the Rock Hall terminus. The ferry was advertised by Abram Ayres in 1769. An Abram Ayres bought land on Swan Creek in April 1744, *Kent County Land Records, Liber 6, 1742–1744, J.S.,* 531. Swan Creek enters the bay at Gratitude, a section of Rock Hall. Nineteenth-century ferries docked at Gratitude. One can surmise this was the case earlier, in the eighteenth century.

7. Hunter Dickinson Farish, ed., *Journal and Letters of Philip Vickers Fithian*, 145. The race course is not identified, but a popular one was located

at Ellendale on the bay, a few miles south of present-day Rock Hall, Maryland.

8. Maryland State Archives, *Index: Maryland State Government Papers, Red Book Series* [Revolutionary War Records: 1775–1789], Vol.II. (Annapolis: MSA) 1484.

9. J. Hall Pleasants, ed., *Archives of Maryland, XLVII, Journal and Correspondence of State Council, 1781* (1930): 226.

CHAPTER 7. Upper Bay Ferries

1. Paul Wilstach, *Tidewater Maryland*, 189. The list was part of a report prepared by the British War Board, May 1778, and filed with the Cornwallis papers.

2. Susan Q. Stranahan, *Susquehanna: River of Dreams*, (Baltimore: Johns Hopkins University Press, 1995), 46.

3. Ibid., 55.

4. A copy of the *York Weekly Advertiser* in the *Pennsylvania Chronicle*, December 19, 1787, gives an account of the controversy.

5. Susan Q. Stranahan, *Susquehanna: River of Dreams*, 48.

6. Ibid., 20.

7. William Hand Browne, ed., *Archives of Maryland, XX, Proceedings of the Council of Maryland, 1693–1696/7* (1900): 320.

8. G. E. Gifford Jr., ed., *Cecil County, Maryland, 1608–1850*, 45, 85–96.

9. Ibid., 58.

10. John Rodgers became the progenitor of a well-known Navy family. His son was Commodore John Rodgers, a hero of the War of 1812. Christopher P. R. Rodgers was commandant of the U.S. Naval Academy during the Civil War, and Lt. John Rodgers, was to become the second U.S. Navy pilot. See Clara Ann Simmons, *The Story of the U.S. Naval Academy* (Annapolis: Naval Institute Press, 1995), 28, 79. Rodgers Tavern fell into disrepair in the late eighteenth century. It was bought in 1950 by the Society for the Preservation of Maryland Antiquities, which restored the building with state aid and cooperation of the Friends of Rodgers Tavern. It is now owned by the town of Perryville and open to the public. *Cecil Whig*, January 20, 1995.

11. C. Milton Wright, *Our Harford Heritage* (n.c., n.p.,n.d), 363.

12. Ibid., 368.

13. Paul Wilstach, *Tidewater Maryland*, 189–90.

14. Mederic-Louis-Elie Moreau de Saint-Méry was born in Quebec in 1750 and became active in the French Revolution. He came to America when anti-French feelings were rampant. President John Adams had him listed as "undesirable," and de Saint Méry returned home. G. E. Gifford Jr., ed., *Cecil County, Maryland, 1608–1850*, 109–12.

CHAPTER 8. Railroad and Automobile Ferries

1. Frances Ann "Fanny" Kemble (1809–1893) was a famous British actress. Matilda Houstoun (1815–1852) was an English woman who traveled in America. She went by rail from Philadelphia to Baltimore and published a book about her travels in 1850. G. E. Gifford Jr., ed., *Cecil County, Maryland, 1608–1850)*, 147, 153.

2. Clara Ann Simmons, *The Story of the U. S. Naval Academy* (Annapolis: Naval Institute Press, 1995), 30.

3. George H. Burgess and Miles C. Kennedy, *Centennial History of the Pennsylvania Railroad Company, 1846–1946* (Philadelphia: Pennsylvania Railroad Co., 1949) 393.

4. John C. Hayman, *Rails along the Chesapeake: A History of Railroading on the Delmarva Peninsula, 1827–1978* (n.c.: Marvadel Publishers, 1979), 72.

5. Ibid., 75.

6. "New Cape Charles Ferry Service to Begin Saturday," *Virginian-Pilot*, March 30, 1933, Part 1:8.

7. Alexander C. Brown, "The End of Virginia's Eastern Shore Ferries," *The Daily Press*, Newport News-Hampton, Virginia, March 22, 1964.

8. John C. Hayman, *Rails Along the Chesapeake*, 125.

9. Ibid., 165.

10. Dickson J. Preston, *Oxford: The First Three Centuries* (Easton, MD: Historical Society of Talbot County, 1984), 14.

11. Ibid., 52.

12. Information on the Claiborne-Annapolis Ferry Company is based on the B. Frank Sherman scrapbooks and the Vertical Files of the Chesapeake Bay Maritime Museum, St. Michaels, Maryland.

13. B. Frank Sherman, "The First Ferry on the Bay," *Baltimore Sunday Sun*, July 27, 1952.

14. *Centreville Observer*, Vol. 67:8, July 3, 1930, 1.

Bibliography

Abbot, W.W., and Dorothy Twohig, eds. *The Papers of George Washington Colonial Series*, Vols. 1, 7, 8, 9. Charlottesville: University Press of Virginia, 1994.

Alexander, Edwin P. *The Pennsylvania Railroad. A Pictorial History*. New York, NY: Bonanza Books, 1967.

Andrews, Matthew Page. *Virginia the Old Dominion*. Garden City, NY: Doubleday, Doran and Company, 1937.

Anne Arundel County Levy Book. Annapolis: n.p., 1811–1836.

Barbour, Philip. L. *The Three Worlds of Captain John Smith*. Boston: Houghton Mifflin Company, 1964.

———. ed. *The Complete Works of Captain John Smith (1580–1631)*. Chapel Hill: University of North Carolina Press, 1986.

Barr, Lockwood. "William Faris, 1728–1804." *Maryland Historical Magazine* 36 (December 1941) 420–39.

Bear, James A., Jr. & Lucia C. Stanton, eds. *The Papers of Thomas Jefferson, Second Series, Jefferson's Memorandum Books*. Princeton: Princeton University Press, 1997.

Beebe, Clarence Lee. "A History of the Chesapeake Bay Ferries to Virginia's Eastern Shore Prior to the Civil War." Master's thesis, University of Richmond, 1954.

Beirne, Francis F. *Baltimore, A Picture History*. Baltimore: Bodine & Associates, 1968.

Beitzell, Edwin W. *Life on the Potomac River*. Baltimore: Abell, 1968.

Blackford, John. *Ferry Hill Plantation Journal, January 4, 1838–January 15, 1839*. Edited by Fletcher M. Green. Chapel Hill: University of North Carolina Press, 1961.

Blair, Carvel Hall and Willits Dyer Ansel. *Chesapeake Bay Notes and Sketches*. Cambridge, MD: Tidewater Publishers, 1970.

Blumgart, Pamela James, ed. *At the Head of the Bay*. Elkton, MD: The Cecil Historical Trust, 1996.

Boltz, Shirley V. *An Account of the Bustling Eighteenth Century Port of Annapolis*. Annapolis: The Liberty Tree, 1975.

Boyd, Thomas. *Poor John Fitch*. New York: G.P. Putnam's Sons, 1935.

Boylan, Henry. *A Dictionary of Irish Biography*. New York: Barnes & Noble Books, 1978.

Breen, T. H. "The Bumpy Path to a New Republic." *New York Times* (February 14, 1999).

Brooks, James W. "George Washington's Travels." Washington, DC: American Highway Educational Bureau, 1932.

Brown, Alexander G. "The End of Virginia's Eastern Shore Ferries." *The Daily Press* (March 22, 1964).

Brown, Jack D. et al. *Charles County Maryland, A History*. South Hackensack, NJ: Custombook, 1976.

Browne, William H. (1883–1912), Clayton C. Hall (1913–1915), Bernard C. Steiner (1916–1927), and J. Hall Pleasants (1929–1938), eds. *Archives of Maryland*, 59 Volumes. Baltimore: Maryland Historical Society.

Brugger, Robert J. *Maryland, A Middle Temperament 1624–1980*. Baltimore: Johns Hopkins University Press in association with Maryland Historical Society, 1989.

Burgess, George H. and Miles C. Kennedy. *Centennial History of the Pennsylvania Railroad Company, 1846–1946*. Philadelphia: Pennsylvania Railroad Co., 1949.

Burgess, Robert H. *Chesapeake Circle*. Cambridge, MD: Cornell Maritime Press, 1965.

———— and H. Graham Wood. *Steamboats Out of Baltimore*. Centreville, MD: Tidewater Publishers, 1968.

Carmer, Carl. *The Susquehanna*. New York: Rinehart and Co., 1955.

Carr, Lois Green, Philip D. Morgan and Jean B. Russo, eds. *Colonial Chesapeake Society*. Chapel Hill: University of North Carolina Press, 1988.

Carter, Edwin C., III, John C. Van Horne and Charles E. Brownell, eds. *Latrobe's View of America, 1795–1820, Selections from Watercolors and Sketches*. New Haven, CT: Yale University Press, 1985.

Clark, Charles B., ed. *The Eastern Shore of Maryland and Virginia*. New York: Lewis Historical Publishing Co., 1950.

Collings, Francis d'A. *The Discovery of the Chesapeake Bay*. St. Michaels, MD: Chesapeake Bay Maritime Museum, 1988.

Cooper, Richard M. *Portrait of Salisbury, Maryland through the 1900s*. Baltimore: Gateway Press, 1944.

Corddry, George H. *Wicomico County History*. Salisbury, MD: Peninsula Press, 1981.

Crisman, Kevin J. and Arthur B. Cohn. *When Horses Walked on Water*. Washington, DC: Smithsonian Institution Press, 1998.

Dabney, Virginius. *Virginia The New Dominion*. Garden City, NY: Doubleday and Company, 1971.

Davidson, Marshall B. "Voyage Pittoresque Aux Etats-Unis de l'Amérique, Paul Svignine En 1811, 1812 et 1813." *American Heritage* XV (1964): 49–63.

Dowell, Susan Stiles. "London Town Publik House and Gardens." *Maryland Magazine* (Spring 1989): 1–64.

Durrenberger, Joseph Austin. *Turnpikes: A Study of the Toll Road Movement in the Middle Atlantic States and Maryland*. Cos Cob, CT: John E. Edwards, 1968.

Eller, Ernest McNeil, ed. *The Chesapeake Bay in the American Revolution*. Centreville, MD: Tidewater Publishers, 1981.

Eighmey, Kathleen M. *The Beach*. Virginia Beach: The Virginia Beach Public Library, 1996.

Emory, Frederic. *Queen Anne's County, Maryland, Its Early History and Development*. Baltimore: The Maryland Historical Society, 1950.

Farish, Hunter Dickinson, ed. *Journal and Letters of Philip Vickers Fithian, 1773–1774, A Plantation Tutor of the Old Dominion*. Williamsburg: Colonial Williamsburg, Inc., 1943.

Fitzpatrick, John C. *George Washington, Colonial Traveler, 1732–1775*. Indianapolis: Bobbs-Merrill Co., 1927.

———. ed. *Writings of George Washington from the Original Manuscript Sources 1745–1799*. Washington, DC: U. S. Government Printing Office, 1931.

Footner, Hulbert. *Rivers of the Eastern Shore*. New York: Farrar & Rinehart Inc., 1944.

Gamst, Frederick C., ed. *Early American Railroads*. Stanford, CA: Stanford University Press,1997.

Gifford, G.E., Jr., ed. *Cecil County Maryland 1608–1850*. Rising Sun, MD: 1974.

Giles, Ted. *Patty Cannon, Woman of Mystery*. Easton, MD: Easton Publishing Company, 1965.

Gottschalk, Louis. *Lafayette and the Close of the American Revolution*. Chicago: University of Chicago Press, 1942.

Gould, Clarence P. *Money and Transportation in Maryland 1720–1765*. Baltimore: Johns Hopkins University Press, 1915.

Greene, Jack P., ed. *The Diary of Colonel Landon Carter of Sabine Hall: 1752–1778*. Charlottesville: University Press of Virginia, 1965.

Gutheim, Frederick. *Illustrated Rivers of America: The Potomac*. New York: Grosset and Dunlap Publishers, 1968.

Hammack, Tennyson Evans. "The Sunny Bank Ferry." *The Bulletin of the Northumberland County Historical Society* (December 1984).

Hammett, Regina Combs. *History of St. Mary's County, Maryland.* Leonardtown, MD: St. Mary's County Bicentennial Comm., 1977.

Hancock, Harold. *The History of Nineteenth Century Laurel.* Westerville, Ohio: Laurel Historical Society, 1983.

Hawthorne, Hildegarde. *Williamsburg Old and New.* New York: D. Appleton Century Company, 1941.

Hayman, John C. *Rails Along the Chesapeake. A History of Railroading on the Delmarva Peninsula 1827–1978.* N.c.: Marvadel Publishers, 1979.

Hienton, Louise Joyner. *Prince George's Heritage.* Baltimore: Maryland Historical Society, 1972.

Holly, David C. *Chesapeake Steamboats, Vanished Fleet.* Centreville, MD: Tidewater Publishers, 1994

Howe, Henry. *Historical Collections of Virginia.* Charleston, SC: Babcock & Co., 1846.

Howard, George W. *Baltimore, the Monumental City, its Past History and Present Resources.* Baltimore: J.D. Ehlen and Company, 1873.

Hudnall, Ada K. *The Great Wicomico Ferry.* Northern Neck of Virginia Historical Magazine (XXI), n.y.

Jackson, Donald & Dorothy Twohig, eds. *The Diaries of George Washington.* Charlottesville: University Press of Virginia, 1979.

Jacob, John E. Jr. *Salisbury and Wicomico County, A Pictorial History.* Virginia Beach: Donning Company, 1981.

Jacobs, Charles and Marian Waters. "Colonel Elijah Viers White." *The Montgomery County Story.* The Montgomery County Historical Society. 22 (Feb. 1979).

Jay, Peter A., ed. *Havre de Grace, An Informal History.* N.c.: Susquehanna Publishing Co., 1986.

Johnston, George. *History of Cecil County, Maryland.* Elkton, MD: Genealogical Publishing Co., 1881.

Jones, Elias. *New Revised History of Dorchester County, Maryland.* Cambridge, MD: Tidewater Publishers, 1960.

Keith, Robert C. *Baltimore Harbor: A Pictorial History.* Baltimore: Ocean World Publishing Co., 1982.

Kent, James. "A New Yorker in Maryland: 1793 and 1821." *Maryland Historical Magazine* (1952): 135–45.

Klapthor, Margaret Brown and Paul Dennis Brown. *The History of Charles County, Maryland.* La Plata, MD: Charles County Tercentenary, Inc., 1958.

Land, Aubrey C., ed. *Archives of Maryland LXXI, Journal and Correspondence of the State Council of Maryland, 1784–1789.* Baltimore: Maryland Historical Society, 1970.

Lincoln, Anna T. *Wilmington, Delaware, Three Centuries under Four Flags.* Rutland, VT: Turtle Publishing Co., 1937.

McMaster, Richard and Ray Eldon Herbert. *A Grateful Remembrance. The Story of Montgomery County, Maryland.* Rockville, MD: Montgomery County Government and Montgomery County Historical Society, 1976.

Mariner, Kirk. *Off 13, The Eastern Shore of Virginia Guidebook*. New Church, VA: Miona Publications, 1987.

Marye, William B. "Early Settlers of the Site of Havre de Grace." *Maryland Historical Magazine* (1918): 135–145.

Maryland, A Guide to the Old Line State. 5th ed. New York: Oxford University Press, 1948.

Maryland State Archives, *Index: Maryland State Government Papers*, Red Book Series [Revolutionary War Records: 1775–1789], Vols. I, II, IV. MSA 1484. Annapolis: Maryland State Archives.

Mereness, Newton D. *Maryland as a Proprietary Province*. New York: MacMillan Company, 1901.

Middleton, Arthur Pierce. *Tobacco Coast, A Maritime History of Chesapeake Bay in the Colonial Era*. Baltimore: Johns Hopkins University Press and the Maryland State Archives, 1984.

Miller, Alice E. *Cecil County Maryland, A Study in Local History*. Elkton, MD: C & L Printing & Specialty Co., 1949.

Miller, Mary R. *Place Names of the Northern Neck of Virginia*. Richmond, VA: Virginia State Library, 1983.

Miller, T. Michael. *Ferries*. [Lecture, n.d.]

Mills, Eric. *Chesapeake Bay in the Civil War*. Centreville, MD: Tidewater Publishers, 1996.

Owens, Hamilton. *Baltimore on the Chesapeake*. Garden City, NY: Doubleday, Doran & Company, 1941.

Papenfuse, Edward C. *In Pursuit of Profit*. Baltimore: Johns Hopkins University Press, 1975.

———. *The Annapolis Merchant in the Era of the American Revolution, 1763–1805*. Baltimore: Johns Hopkins University Press, 1975.

Paullin, Charles Oscar. *Commodore John Rodgers, Captain, Commodore, and Senior Officer of the American Navy 1773–1838*. Cleveland: N.p., 1910.

Perry, James R. *The Formation of a Society on Virginia's Eastern Shore 1615–1655*. Chapel Hill: University of North Carolina Press, 1990.

Pleasants, J. Hall, ed. *Archives of Maryland LIII, Proceedings of the County Court of Charles County 1658–1666*. Baltimore: Maryland Historical Society.

Porter, Frank W., III. *Indians in Maryland and Delaware, A Critical Bibliography*. Bloomington, IN: Indiana University Press, 1979.

Posey, John Thornton. "The Improvident Ferryman of Mt. Vernon, the Trials of Capt. John Posey." *Virginia Cavalcade* (Summer 1989).

Presnall, Clifford C. "Ferries of the Northern Neck of Virginia." *Northern Neck of Virginia Historical Magazine* (1979), 3258–3281.

Preston, Dickson J. *Oxford, the First Three Centuries*. Easton, MD: The Historical Society of Talbot County, 1984.

Reps, John W. *Tidewater Towns, City Planning in Colonial Virginia and Maryland*. Williamsburg: Colonial Williamsburg Foundation, 1972.

Ridgely, David. *Annals of Annapolis*. Baltimore: Cushing and Brother, 1841.

Rodgers, William. "Riding the Maryland Rails, Part 1: Central Maryland Where it All Began." *Maryland Magazine.* (Summer 1987): 39–42.

Rock Hall Historical Collection. Rock Hall, MD: Rock Hall Commemoration, 1957.

Rouse, Parke, Jr. *The Great Wagon Road.* New York: McGraw-Hill Book Company, 1973.

Rowland, Kate Mason. *The Life of George Mason, 1752–1792.* New York: G. P. Putnam's Sons, 1892.

Rukert, Norman G. *Historic Canton: Baltimore's Industrial Heartland and its People.* Baltimore: Bodine & Associates, 1978.

Sandler, Gilbert. "Few Remember Life Before the Bridge." *Maryland Magazine,* Summer 1983: 2–9.

Scharf, J. Thomas. *History of Delaware 1609–1888.* Philadelphia: L.J. Richards & Company, 1888.

———. *History of Baltimore City and County.* Philadelphia: Louis H. Everts, 1881.

Schlerf, Gary W. *History of the Canton Railroad Company: Artery of Baltimore's Industrial Heartland.* Baltimore: The Company, 1996.

Selckman, August. "The Susquehanna, Mother of the Chesapeake." *Maryland Magazine* (Autumn 1990), 6–17.

Sherman, B. Frank. "The First Ferry on the Bay." *Baltimore Sunday Sun* (July 27, 1952).

Shriver, J. Alexis. *Lafayette in Harford County, Memorial Monograph 1781–1931.* Bel Air, MD: Privately Printed, 1931.

Simmons, Clara Ann. *The Story of the U.S. Naval Academy.* Annapolis: Naval Institute Press, 1995.

Sommerville, Mollie. *Washington Walked Here.* Washington, DC: Acropolis Books, 1970.

Stanton, Richard L. *Potomac Journey: Fairfax Stone to Tidewater.* Washington, DC: Smithsonian Institution Press, 1993.

Stevens, William Oliver. *Old Williamsburg and Her Neighbors.* New York: Dodd, Mead & Company, 1938.

Stover, John F. *History of the Baltimore and Ohio Railroad.* West Lafayette, IN: Purdue University Press, 1987.

Stranahan, Susan Q. *Susquehanna, River of Dreams.* Baltimore: Johns Hopkins University Press, 1995.

Struthers, Burt. *Philadelphia Holy Experiment.* Garden City, NY: Doubleday, Doran and Company, 1945.

Tazewell, William L. *Norfolk's Waters, An Illustrated Maritime History of Hampton Roads.* Woodland Hills, CA: Windsor Publications, 1982.

The State of Maryland Historical Atlas. Washington, DC: Raymond, Parish, Pine & Plavnich, December 1973.

Tilghman, Oswald. *History of Talbot County, Maryland 1661–1861.* Baltimore: Williams & Wilkins Company, 1915.

Tilp, Frederick. *The Chesapeake Bay of Yore, Mainly about Rowing and Sailing Craft.* Annapolis: Chesapeake Bay Foundation, 1982.

————. *Chesapeake Fact, Fiction & Fun*. Bowie, MD: Heritage Books, 1988.

————. "Tidewater Tales" in *Chesapeake Skipper*, August 1952.

Travers, Paul J. *The Patapsco, Baltimore's River of History*. Centreville, MD: Tidewater Publishers, 1990.

Truitt, Charles J. *Breadbasket of the Revolution, Delmarva in the War for Independence*. Salisbury, MD: Historical Books, 1975.

Truitt, Reginald V. *Kent Island, Maryland's Oldest Settlement*. Stevensville, MD: Women of Christ Church, 1965.

Turman, Nora Miller. *The Eastern Shore of Virginia 1603–1964*. Onancock, VA: Eastern Shore News, 1964.

Tyler, Lyon G., ed. "William Gregory's Journal from Fredericksburg, Virginia to Philadelphia, 30th of September 1765 to 11th October 1765." *William and Mary Quarterly* 13, 224–226.

Van Horn, R. Lee. *Out of the Past - Prince Georgians and Their Land*. Riverdale, MD: Prince George's County Historical Society, 1976.

Vaughan, Alden T. *American Genesis: Captain John Smith and the Founding of Virginia*. Boston: Little, Brown and Company, 1975.

Virginia, A Guide to the Old Dominion, American Guide Series. New York: Oxford University Press, 1940.

Vojtech, Pat. "Pace of the Past." *Maryland Magazine*. Summer 1987: 6–15.

Walker, Carroll. *Carroll Walker's Norfolk, A Tricentennial Pictorial History*. Virginia Beach: Donning Co., 1981.

Wayland, John W. *The Washingtons and Their Homes*. Baltimore: Genealogical Publishing Co., 1998.

Weeks, Christopher, ed. "Maryland Historical Trust Inventory of Historic Sites, Caroline County." Annapolis: Maryland Historical Trust, 1980.

Weigley, Russel F., ed. *Philadelphia, a 300 Year History*. New York: W. W. Norton and Company, 1982.

Wertenbaker, Thomas Jefferson. *The Old South. The Founding of American Civilization*. New York: Charles Scribner's Sons, 1942.

————. *Norfolk, Historic Southern Port*. Durham, NC: Duke University Press, 1962.

Williams, Carroll E. "Harbor Ferries Ran for 125 Years" *Baltimore Sun*, August 9, 1952.

Wilson, John C. *Virginia's Northern Neck*. Norfolk, VA: The Donning Company, 1984.

Wilstach, Paul. *Potomac Landings*. New York: Tudor Publishing Company, 1937.

————. *Tidewater Maryland*. Indianapolis, IN: Bobbs-Merrill Company, 1931.

————. *Tidewater Virginia*. Indianapolis, IN: Bobbs-Merrill Company, 1929.

Wright, C. Milton. "Our Harford Heritage: A History of Harford County, Maryland." N.c., n.p., 1967.

Wright, Sarah Bird. *Ferries of America, A Guide to Adventurous Travel*. Atlanta: Peachtree Publishers, 1987.

Vertical Files

Cecil County Historical Society, Elkton, MD
Chesapeake Bay Maritime Museum, St. Michaels, MD
Columbia Historic Preservation Society, Columbia, PA
Eastern Shore Public Library, Accomac, VA
Historical Society of Harford County, Bel Air, MD
The Mariners' Museum, Newport News, VA
Maryland Historical Society, Baltimore, MD
Queen Anne's County Free Library, Centreville, MD
Westmoreland County Museum and Library, Montross, VA

Newspapers

Alexandria Gazette
Baltimore Sun
Centreville Observer
Chestertown Apollo
Maryland Gazette
Newport News-Hampton Daily Press
Norfolk Ledger-Dispatch
Norfolk Virginian-Pilot
Virginia Gazette

Illustrations

Chapter 3

Chapter 4

Chapter 5

Chapter 6

Chapter 7

Chapter 8

Index